REVIEWS

"In **The Long Road Home,** hard-core biker Bryan Hall relates the stories about having endured some s**t. Some serious s**t. A terrible accident (a de facto hit-and-run, really) that fractured fifteen (15!) vertebrae along with numerous other fractures and broken bones. Add to all that a cop with a heavy bias against bikers, a slack legal system, surgeries, and waiting forever for reparations. (It goes on and on.)

Any biker, just about, who had gone through all that would have given up on the motorcycle thing. Given up on a lot of other things as well. Not Hall. He's as dedicated to biking (i.e. Freedom) as ever.

The Long Road Home is about other things as well. It's a refreshing, intimate and inspirational memoir. It's engaging travel literature. (He covers so much of the United States.) It's jam-packed with historical information along with broad statements on the intrinsic values of the United States and Freedom and the Liberty to choose our own paths. Yes. It's all that."

- Foster Kinn, author of the bestselling **Freedom's Rush** *books*

"Once you pick it up, the only reason you'll want to put this book down is to hop on your scoot and go for a ride! Bryan made me feel like I was along on the journey as he expertly blends a wonderfully detailed travel journal with an intimate glimpse into his personal resurgence after a life-changing wreck. If you ride, his stories will inspire you to hit the throttle and go exploring, maybe even some of the destinations he so eloquently describes. If you don't ride...what are you waiting for?"

- Elaine Smith

"From the first chapter, this book captured my attention and held it throughout, with humor, shock, and even history lessons. His stories truly embody the joy of riding and the life of a biker, both good and bad."

- M. Phillips

"What a great story! From the challenges to the triumphs, Hall weaves a captivating story of life on the road and the dangers that riders face daily. His determination and passion for riding is plain to see on every page, and his fearlessness in calling out the injustices that bikers often face is inspirational. This book is a must read for riders of all types!"

- Justin Evans

Published 2021 by Banyan Tree Press, an imprint of Hugo House Publishers, Ltd.

ISBN: 978-1-948261-64-7
Library of Congress Control Number: 2021923097

Design: Christa Mella
Cover Photo: Laura Hartsock

BANYAN · TREE · PRESS

Published 2021 by Banyan Tree Press,
an imprint of Hugo House Publishers, Ltd.
Denver Colorado, Austin Texas.

BRYAN HALL

THE LONG ROAD HOME

BANYAN · TREE · PRESS
an imprint of
Hugo House Publishing, Ltd.
Denver Colorado, Austin Texas

CONTENTS

To Jennifer & Shannon for making me the proudest
Dad on the planet. You girls rock!

THE LONG ROAD HOME

CHAPTER ONE

32 years. 5 motorcycles. Well over 250,000 miles.

That's how long it had been since my last motorcycle crash. I have ridden in cities, in deserts, over mountains, on beaches, through farmland, rangelands and wheat fields. I remember an old greybeard biker telling me, when I first started riding, that there are two kinds of bikers: those that have crashed, and those that will.

My last crash, 32 years ago, was caused by an old lady turning left in front of me in broad daylight. My Yamaha 650 Special hit her car broadside and flipped onto the trunk. Luckily, I saw it coming in time to slow the bike, gear down and jump off. I suffered a few bruises, some scraped up boots, and a tear in my jacket. The bike was totaled. Of course, she said she "didn't see" me.

In the following decades, I rode almost everywhere that time, money, and weather would allow. In 2004 I bought my first new bike, a Harley Davidson Wide Glide. I put 23,000 miles on it in 20 months. As much as I loved that bike, I knew I needed something bigger for the way I was riding; so, in February of 2006 I bought a new 2006 Road King with 7 miles on it.

The more miles I put on that Road King, the more I loved it. If it was not snowing or icy out, chances are I was in the saddle. In the ensuing years, I went all over Oregon, Washington, British Columbia,

Montana; to California, Sturgis, and across the country and back. The cross-country trip became my first book, "Life Behind Bars," which detailed the six-week, almost 10,000-mile journey to the Atlantic Ocean and back. I loved being on the road so much that I wanted to share my experiences with other people, and started my own website, hiwayflyer.com. Many of my other trips are chronicled there, as well as in numerous motorcycle magazines.

Fast forward to 2016…February 20, 2016, to be exact, approximately 176,000 miles after buying the Road King.

I had decided to go for a lunch ride with some friends since the day was decent. "Decent" for February in the Pacific Northwest meant mild temperatures and no rain. It had rained overnight so the roads were still partially wet, but otherwise it was a nice day with temperatures in the mid-50s. I had a passenger, Laura, on the back of my scoot, and friends Kevin and Christine were on his bike. We headed out of Tacoma toward the small town of Enumclaw in the Cascade foothills and stopped for lunch and a beer at a place called the Yella Beak. A couple of hours later we were back on the bikes, headed toward home on the freeway. There was traffic, but it wasn't heavy, and we were moving along with no problems.

None, that is, until we noticed a white Audi making his way in and out of traffic and presumably trying to get ahead of everyone. The Audi driver weaved around, got in front of us and slowed down. This kind of thing happens a lot, so I signaled to change lanes and keep moving. The Audi driver sped up and did it again, not once but a few times.

By now I was realizing this guy was a threat, so I changed lanes *(into the passing lane)*, throttled up and got away from him. At this point he was quite a way behind us, and we settled in for the ride. Kevin was in the next lane over as he was going to jump off the freeway at the next exit, and I was still in the left lane. Out of nowhere, the Audi comes blasting up next to me, cut into my lane and hit his brakes. No, there was no one in front of him to cause him to hit the binders, but because he had cut me off, I had to react.

Every biker knows about the "escape route." When riding, you always have to keep an eye open for a way out of a situation. Most of the time, thinking about it is not an option, and can actually be deadly. It becomes a gut reaction or reflex, learned by years and miles of riding.

My only feasible escape route was to go left, onto the shoulder. Hitting my own brakes hard enough to stop would have propelled us into his trunk, going right would have meant clipping the Audi's back right and then hitting the car in the next lane. Going left was the instantaneous and reasonable route, so I did…onto the shoulder, with rumble strips and a cable barrier (*or, as bikers call it, a cheese slicer*). The rumble strips were filled with water from the previous nights' rain. Once on the shoulder, I was just letting off the throttle when I saw the driver of the Audi look at me in his mirror, and swerve to the left, hitting my bike with the left rear fender of his car.

At 65 or so miles per hour.

On purpose.

I don't remember hitting the cables, but I do know that in the ensuing seconds, I took out 150 feet of cable barrier before my Road King got tangled up and threw Laura and me another 150 feet or so into the grassy median. I do remember hitting the ground, on my back, with a thump. Man, did that hurt. I could hear Laura screaming, and wanted to get up and check on her; but there were people all around me telling me to stay still, help was on the way, don't move, and so on. *(One of the first persons at my side was a fellow rider and former paramedic. She made sure I stayed put!)* Then the paramedics were there, doing what they do best: assessing the damage, asking me questions, getting me into an ambulance. Of course, State Patrol was there too, and the first question they asked me was "have you been drinking?" Not, "what happened," but had I been drinking?

Paramedics working on the injured

13

The guy who just tried to kill us was sitting in his car, after initially trying to flee the scene. He had been stopped by other motorists and refused to get out of the car. The Police questioned him and found out he had been up at a local casino, watching a NASCAR race in the bar. Other witnesses said he was driving aggressively even before he encountered us, and in their infinite wisdom and ultimate professionalism, the Washington State Patrol let him go home. They did not ask him if he had been drinking, did not administer a field sobriety test, did not even write him a ticket. But more on that later.

As it turns out, there was a large charity run for another biker that day, one of the local ABATE chapter presidents, and the site of the crash was along the route of their run. Literally dozens of bikes rolled by as we were being tended to by the paramedics. Because my bike at the time was not your cookie-cutter Harley, it was almost instantly recognizable, and due to the severity of the crash, initial rumors began floating through the riding community that our crash was fatal. It very nearly was. What added fuel to that rumor was the emergency responders had erected a shield of sorts to keep the drivers from seeing us lying in the median. Typically, that is done in a fatality crash, but for us it was because most of our clothes had been torn off or removed by the medical personnel so they could assess our injuries and treat us… yes, we were lying in the median pretty much stark ass nekkid *(now I know why my Mom always said to wear clean underwear!)*.

The ride to the hospital in the ambulance was bumpy, chaotic, and painful. I was able, with the help of the paramedics, to get word to one of my daughters of the crash and where I was headed. Once in the Trauma Center, I was surrounded by medical personnel trying to assess my injuries and get me stabilized. I was bleeding internally, but they did not know from where. While the medicos were figuring out how severe my injuries were and why I was bleeding, the alleged "Drug Recognition Expert" from the Washington State Patrol was telling me he was going to perform a field sobriety test on me. Being the smartass that I am, I remember telling him that it might be kind of tough, as I was strapped to a gurney. He said there was another type of field test they could do, and he told me to close my eyes and count off thirty seconds. Evidently, I determined that thirty seconds was actually twenty-five seconds. What exactly that meant, I still do not know, but since I was being pumped full of God knows what drugs at the time; I think I'm lucky I just didn't pass out. Next, he said he was going to take my blood, and I again remember telling him, "Go ahead, everyone else is."

At this point he said that since he had obtained a telephone search warrant for the retrieval of my blood, he was going to read me my rights, to "protect me." He never told me I was under arrest; and listening to the transcripts of his subsequent telephone calls to the dispatcher, he couldn't honestly say that he placed me under arrest. He hemmed and hawed and stumbled all over himself, then told the dispatcher, "Well, he understood he was." Dude, I was so far in LaLa Land at that point from the pain and the medications, I could barely understand English. *(By the way, my blood test came back with NO alcohol in my system at all.)*

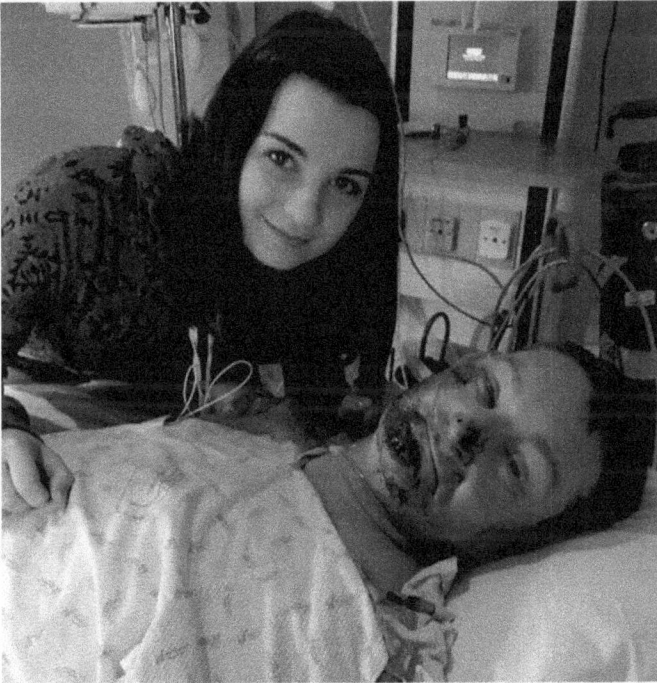

In ICU with my granddaughter

Meanwhile, the docs finally determined that since I was bleeding internally, they needed to perform surgery to find out exactly what was bleeding. In addition to the blood loss, I had also suffered a burst fracture of my L-2 vertebrae *(that's a nice way of saying it basically exploded)*, fractured fourteen other vertebrae, fractured all my ribs, broke a small bone in my left wrist known as a hyoid, and broke my left ankle, not to mention five broken bones in my left foot, and broke the small toe on my left foot. Oh, and let's not forget the road rash on my face, arm, and shoulder. I was wheeled into surgery, where they fused my spine from my T-12 through L-4 vertebrae—essentially my entire lumbar section. Two titanium rods and numerous titanium screws were used to secure everything in place. They also were able to stop the internal bleeding, but not before giving me numerous transfusions. In the words of the surgeon, the surgery was a success and went "well." In other words, I didn't die, and I was not paralyzed. Which, honestly, was a miracle considering I had been pushed into a cable barrier and was tossed through the air for 150 feet before landing. I spent four days in the Intensive Care Unit, and then was transferred to a general care unit, where I spent the next fourteen days. A few days after being transferred, I had surgery on my wrist to repair the broken hyoid bone by inserting another small titanium screw to hold it all together.

CHAPTER TWO

I do have to say, the staff at the hospital took excellent care of me. Hell, even the food was good, when I wasn't on any dietary restrictions, anyway. The downside, however, was that I could not walk, as my left foot and my left wrist were in stages of recovery, and therefore I was prohibited from putting any weight on them. And, yes, I am left-handed. In addition to all that, they were medicating me with Oxycodone, Dilaudid, and other fun things to manage my pain, every four hours around the clock. Believe me, that pain was unbelievable. Physical therapy started within a few days, and mainly consisted of me trying to walk again. Hobble would be more like it, as I could not put weight on my left side, but I was using a walker set up for just my situation. Standing was the first part, and the first day I was able to stand for twenty-six seconds before I fell back, exhausted. Every day, the therapist would come in and make me get up and *(try to)* walk. Well, "walk" is inaccurate. Since I could not put any weight on my left foot or use my left hand, I was using a walker with a modified left grip. I would stand/lean on the walker, eventually working my way up to walk/hobble/hop to the bathroom…10 feet away. Within about a week, I could maneuver myself out of my room into the hallway and back, about 15 feet. That ten minutes of each day literally wiped me out. I didn't know it at the time, but the doctors had told my family when they were going in to do my surgery, that they didn't know if I would ever walk again.

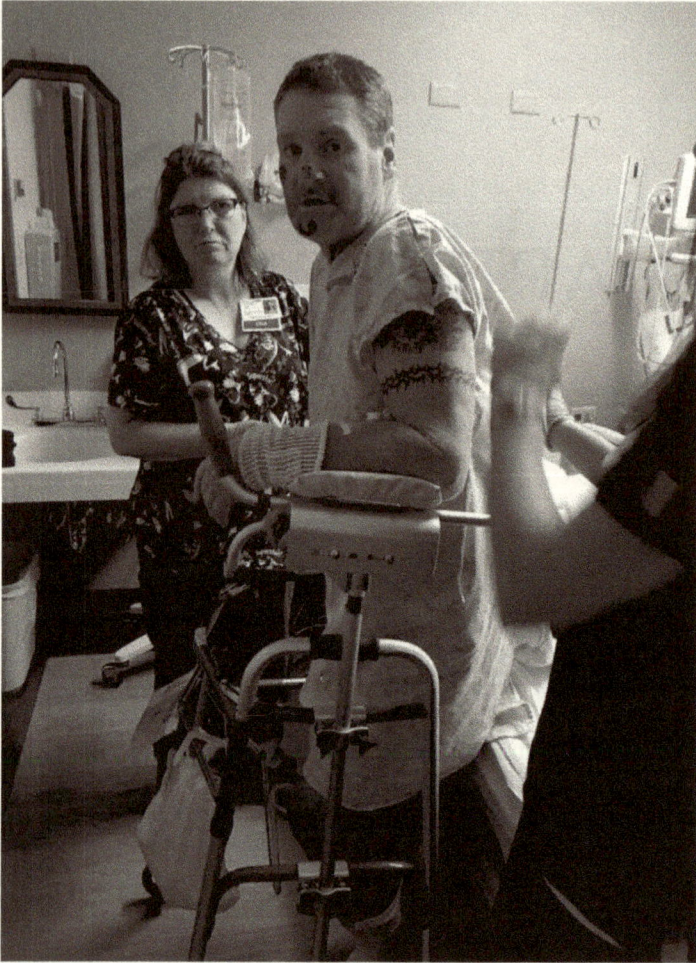

A week after the crash, trying to walk

Up in Seattle, at Harborview Medical Center, Laura was undergoing her own version of Hell; her injuries were severe enough that they re-directed her during the ambulance ride from going to Tacoma General to Harborview, the only Level 1 Trauma Center in the State. She was placed into a medical coma for two days. The list of injuries was horrifying: a compound fracture of her right arm, dislocation of her left shoulder, torn left bicep and rotator cuff, broken left fibula *(leg bone)*, shattered left tibia and a pilon fracture *(the part of the tibia near the ankle, also called the shinbone)*, and a shattered left heel. The left Achilles tendon and ankle were "degloved," which is what happens when the top layers of skin are ripped from the muscle and connecting tissue. She underwent two surgeries on her arm and numerous surgeries on her leg. Her heel was so severely damaged that doctors could not repair it, they simply cleaned out the shattered fragments. As a result, to this day she has no heel nor Achilles tendon on her left foot. Due to the severity of her leg injuries, doctors initially thought they were going to have to amputate her leg. Fortunately, they were able to save it, although she lost muscle and tendons as a result. In addition, her left foot is now a half shoe size smaller than her right. Like me, she also had a concussion resulting in a Traumatic Brain Injury.

Surprisingly, she was in the hospital for a total of six days before going home, even though she was still in an external fixator. An "Ex Fix" is a brace-like device that strongly resembles a tinker toy set and was attached to her leg with pins and cables to help keep her bones in place while they heal and grow together. The device needs to be adjusted *(with a wrench...yes, a wrench)* up to six times per day to keep the tension. She likely would have been there longer, but she demanded to be released, and as she worked in the medical field and had someone at home to help her with her recovery, the doctors acquiesced.

I was completely unaware that they had taken her to Harborview, as well as being unaware of her injuries. By the time I did find out, there was a no-contact order in place between the two of us, courtesy of the Pierce County Prosecutor *(more on that in a bit...)*.

Meanwhile, my therapy continued, and they kept pumping medications into me every few hours, twenty-four hours a day: Dilaudid, Oxycodone, Tylenol, and God knows what else. One of the glorious side effects of all the pain medication was constipation. Yes, boys and girls I was plugged, blocked, dammed up so nothing was moving. It's not unusual to get that way from the opioid pain medications, and after a couple of days they decided I needed help. We started out with some mild laxatives, and then moved on to more fun stuff, eventually getting to that ultimate step: the enema. Nothing happened. They tried again, and nothing. Evidently, I was "impacted," meaning shit *(literally)* was so clogged up in there it was packed tight, and nothing was helping to break the proverbial log jam *(no pun intended)*. What happened next, I would not have wished on anybody. Oh, it really didn't bother me much, because I was still pumped full of pain meds. I really felt sorry for that poor nurse who had to do a "digital manipulation." In other words, he had to reach inside and literally dig the crap out. With his finger. Yes, it hurt, but I felt sorrier for him, having to do it. His attitude was, "oh well, no biggie, just part of the job."

And guess what? Still nothing. Nope, no movement at all. Drastic times call for drastic measures, and they decided to do back-to-back enemas…hell, if one was good, two would be better, right? So, they did. I was lying on my side, and when he finished, he said, "When you feel the pressure, just ring. I'll be right outside the door and I'll be here to take you into the bathroom." No sooner had he left the room when I felt it…the tectonic plates were moving. I guess you could say "shit was about to get real," and it did. I rang the bell and yelled, and as he entered my room, everything let go. Days of clogged bowels unloaded, all over my bed and the floor. I was horrified, but the nurses just came in, cleaned me up, moved me and cleaned up my room in no time. The bed in my room was one that performed all kinds of functions, including weighing me. When the staff finally got everything done and got me back into bed, they discovered I had, in the last five minutes, lost over ten pounds. *(I have had people tell me I was full of crap for years, but on this night, I could prove I wasn't!)*

After another ten days or so they determined I could be transferred to a skilled nursing facility. Essentially, a "skilled nursing facility" is a nice name for a nursing home/rehab center. My friends and daughter did some research in the area to decide which one I would go to, and they settled on Orchard Park Healthcare and Rehab Center in Tacoma. Orchard Park was a place that one of the local ABATE Chapters had done a "Santas for Seniors" run a couple of years prior, bringing gifts and cheer to the residents of the facility. The day we did the ride, it was trying its best to rain, and the staff let us bring several bikes into the main hallway. That was a huge hit with the residents! I look back on that run as one of the best charity rides I had done…kind of like a toy run for old folks. The staff also made an impression on a couple of my friends, so when it came time to look for a place for me to go, they remembered Orchard Park and went with my daughter to check it out. The paperwork was filled out, the arrangements made, and I was loaded up in a medical transport for the ride across town.

I honestly think I was the youngest person there. It was my home for six more weeks, until I could walk and function again on my own. Orchard Park was great, and I could not have been in a better facility: the staff was attentive and friendly, the therapists were great, and the room was like staying in a hotel. Since I had no dietary or visitor restrictions, my friends brought me snacks and treats from the "outside." One sunny afternoon, my friend Tammie stopped at a 7-11 on the way to visit and picked up a couple of beers for me and some wine for her so we could sit outside on the patio and visit. The clerk mentioned something about being thirsty, and she said, "oh, I'm taking the beer to my friend in rehab." It was only after she was back in her car that she realized what she had said! Horrified and embarrassed, she even went back inside and explained it was physical rehab, not alcohol rehab, that I was undergoing.

Tammie and one of my other friends, Lori, were my "angels" during my recovery. One or both were at my side every day that I was in the hospital and rehab center. They took turns doing my laundry, keeping my spirits up, communicating with my lawyer, running errands, and pretty much everything else I needed. Once I became more "mobile," they often took me out for a drink or for lunch. Lori even took me into downtown Tacoma one day to get a straight-razor shave at one of the barber shops. When my Mom and brother came from Canada to visit, Lori went over to my house and made sure it was cleaned and fresh sheets were on the beds for them. I could not have done it without them.

I went through physical therapy twice per day for the six weeks I stayed at Orchard Park. As my healing progressed, I was able to walk with help from my walker and eventually a cane, and finally was able to go home. At the time, I was living in a 75-year-old house, with small rooms. In fact, the bathroom was so small that I could not go into it with my walker and turn around. I quite literally had to back into the toilet to conduct my business. Therapists came in twice a week to work with me at home, until I was mobile enough to go to outpatient therapy about a month later. Part of my in-home therapy was to walk. The neighborhood I lived in had sidewalks, and after the initial exercises, we would grab the walker or cane *(depending on how I felt that day)* and head out. At first, I could walk about halfway down the block, about 500 feet before I had to rest, then make my way back. It took about two weeks before I was able to actually make it around the block, a total distance of a third of a mile. In the meantime, the walker got used less and the cane became a necessity. Those walks absolutely wiped me out. After about a month I was up to a mile or so, depending on my pain level and fatigue. The neighborhood was adjacent to one of Tacoma's nicest parks, and there is a lake in the park with a walking trail around it. To walk around the lake completely is one mile. My goal was to be able to walk to the park, around the lake, and back home, a distance of just over two miles. It took a lot of work, but by the end of May I was able to do that a couple of times a week. I made sure I did at least one mile a day, but often pushed myself to go further if I could. I still walk about two miles or so per day, again, depending upon my pain level.

That's not to say I was, or am, "healed." Let's just say I'm as good as I get. Even to this day, chronic pain is my unwelcome companion, and sometimes to the point of laying me low for a day or so. My short-term memory and my attention span are pretty well shot, and fatigue will often sneak up on me to the point where I essentially cannot get off the couch. PTSD and anxiety have reared their ugly heads as a result of the brain injury as well, so loud, crowded spaces are no longer places I want to be.

CHAPTER THREE

Once I was back home, I had an abundance of free time on my hands. I could not do much of anything physical other than my therapy. Being an independent person, I was used to doing everything myself: cleaning house, mowing the lawns, washing my car, and so on. I could not do any of that…even vacuuming was too strenuous. Typically, when I have free time like that, I would watch TV, read, do crossword puzzles, and write. I began to realize that these activities were also now extremely difficult to do. I could turn on the TV, and within a couple of minutes not have any idea what I was watching. Reading was even worse: I have always been a reader, thanks to my Mom. She used to read to my older brother and me when we were little, and taught us to read almost right from the start. When I went into first grade, I was reading at a third-grade level. I love to read, and if a book caught my interest, I could rip through it in no time. Typically, a 300-page book would be devoured in about two days. It was not unusual for me to read two or three books in a week. In the rehab center, however, I could read a page and not remember a damn thing that was on it. The first full book I read after the crash was a 220-page novel…it took me over four weeks to get through it. Writing was also a chore. Writing has always come almost naturally to me. I can take an idea, sit at my desk, and get my thoughts into words almost without effort. During that time,

I tried to write a simple letter, and could not even form the words I wanted. If I tried to sit down to write, not only couldn't I concentrate or focus on what the task was, but the words wouldn't come. No, it wasn't "writer's block", it was that the words would not come to the surface. They were there, I knew what I wanted to say, but I couldn't remember them. That, too, is getting better.

Something was wrong. I couldn't understand it, and it was really bothering me. Once I was out of the rehab center, back home, and mobile once more, I sought out a counselor to see if I could find out what the hell was going on. It didn't take long for Sara, my counselor, to figure out that I was suffering the effects of a Traumatic Brain Injury, or TBI. When I had landed after my 150-foot flight through the air, my head stopped moving, but my brain didn't. It was like a damn pinball, bouncing off the insides of my skull. Further sessions discovered that I also had PTSD, not uncommon in brain injury cases. Evidently, the doctors in the Trauma Center were so focused on my physical injuries and internal bleeding that they understandably missed the head trauma...especially since I was reasonably lucid and responsive in the Emergency Room.

Over the course of many months, Sara helped me to deal not only with the PTSD, but also to mitigate the issues caused by the TBI. Unlike many people experience after traumatic events, I *(thankfully)* was not plagued with nightmares of the crash. I brought that up in one of our meetings, and she explained that it was because I knew beyond any doubt that I had done everything I could have to avoid the crash, and as a result I had no guilt to plague my thoughts. What did happen, though, was that certain things would come out of nowhere and set my mind spinning. One night, I was watching a movie on TV. The lead character was trying to avenge wrongs done to his family and was being chased by the bad guys. In one scene, one of the hoodlums was on a motorcycle, chasing the Dad. The Dad suddenly stopped the car and opened his driver's door, causing the motorcycle to slam into the open door and send the rider flying. I know, typical Hollywood fare *(yeah, I should have seen it coming, but remember, my brain was not working normally yet)*.

As suddenly as that bike hit the car door, I found myself on the floor, curled into a ball, and shaking like a Chihuahua at the North Pole. It took about ten minutes before I calmed down enough to get up and look at the TV...which had somehow been shut off. I poured myself a strong shot of whiskey, and found something else to watch. That incident dominated our next couple of sessions.

I also went to see a psychiatrist to confirm Sara's diagnosis of TBI and PTSD. That was fun. No, he didn't tell me to "lie on the couch and tell me about your Mother" *(you read that in a German accent, didn't you?)*; instead, he gave me a series of small tests and exercises to determine how my memory and thought processes were affected. It took only about a half-hour for him to confirm what we already knew.

The other monster that reared its ugly head during all this was almost crippling anxiety. I've always been kind of a loner, and never worried about doing things alone. After my crash, crowds, noises, and seemingly enclosed spaces would freak me out: my blood pressure would go up, my head would start pounding, and the color would drain from my face.

About five months or so after the crash, I went down to the Las Vegas area to visit some friends. I was supposed to be their best man at their wedding…which took place one week after my crash. Since I obviously hadn't made it for the wedding, I went down to pay them a visit. One day, one of my friends and I took a drive to the Las Vegas strip itself, and even though we were in a car, I was freaking out. The lights, the crowds, the noise, the bustle all over-stimulated me to the point where I was having trouble catching my breath.

Sara's counseling and methods for regaining some semblance of normal were invaluable to me in rebuilding my life, and I still use a lot of the exercises and tips to this day.

CHAPTER FOUR

The initial response from my family, the biker community and friends were amazing----charity runs, Go Fund Me accounts, and overall support for myself and Laura showed us the love and support that only bikers will do for a fallen rider. An almost constant stream of visitors flowed into my hospital room, so many that when a friend came to visit me, he asked at the front desk what room I was in...the receptionist didn't even have to look it up, she knew it by heart from being asked so often. I feel like I need to explain something: I do not ride with a club or organization, I don't have a large number of people I call "friends," and I am kind of a loner. People I did not know came and visited me, offered to help me, prayed for me, and so on. One of the Christian motorcycle groups came in and offered to pray for me. One of the members, after hearing how the crash happened, said "the angels were truly lifting you up that day," meaning that I was still alive after flying through the air for 150 feet. I agree. But I told her I wish they would have set me down a little more gently! I told them that since I was still alive, either God wasn't done with me yet, or the Devil looked up and said, "Oh Hell no...we're not ready for him!"

What I did discover was that a lot of people had either seen the crash happen or drove by right after it happened. In fact, one of the nurses in the Trauma Center received a phone call from her father telling her they were likely getting victims of the crash. He told her he had been driving by and saw me flying through the air and landing. He, too, thought I was dead. A couple of my friends saw the paramedics working on us and my bike suspended in what was left of the cable barrier. They recognized my bike and actually beat me to the hospital!

Our largest charity run was organized by my friend Tammie. It took place on a cloudy Saturday and over 100 bikes showed up. I tagged along *(in a cage, as I was still using a walker)* and watched as the riders and passengers ponied up cash for raffle items, 50/50 tickets, and auction items. This was also the first time I saw Laura since the crash, she was there in a wheelchair. It was, to say the least, an awkward reunion. The charity run was a huge success, with lots of money raised for us; but the best part was seeing the love, support and respect from our community. Every kind of bike and biker were represented, from sport bike riders to one-percenters; and they all opened their hearts and wallets for us.

While I was in the hospital, I interviewed a variety of lawyers, and chose one based out of Kirkland, WA named Max Meyers. Max specializes in motorcycle crashes and claims, and was the most knowledgeable and straight-forward of all the attorneys I consulted. This guy knows his stuff! At one point, I was contacted by the Washington State Patrol, who wanted to interview me and get my statement. I passed the message along to Max, who in turn contacted them and offered to set up an interview time. The Trooper asked Max if he would be there, and Max replied that I would not be interviewed without benefit of counsel. At that point, the Trooper said something to the effect of "never mind," and hung up. They never contacted me again. It's nice to know that the Sixth Amendment is alive and well in Washington.

In July, I found out that our assailant was being charged with two counts of Felony Vehicular Assault. Shockingly, and contrary to what the Pierce County Prosecutor had told my attorney, I was also charged with one count of Felony Vehicular Assault. Why? Because my passenger was injured. *(I later found out that this is standard practice for the Pierce County Prosecutor, if your passenger is injured on your bike for almost any reason, you will be charged.)* The way I discovered I was being charged was by a letter in the mail. The letter was not sent via registered mail, or hand-delivered by a process server or deputy, but just a regular letter. According to the charging papers, I was being charged as a co-conspirator with the guy who tried to kill me. If you ask any lawyer or judge you can find, a person cannot be a victim and a conspirator in the same crime, that's kind of the first thing they teach you in law school. But, in Washington, they don't seem to care about that. My arraignment was scheduled for two days away, so I had to scramble to find and hire a criminal defense attorney. I consulted my friend Elaine, a paralegal for whom I used to do process service, and she recommended a former colleague, Rob Freeby. Contrary to his name, he was in no way "free," in fact, that fee will shock the living crap out of ya! On the other hand, he was totally worth the money I paid him.

I *(obviously)* pleaded not guilty to the charge, and we began the process of "discovery." Discovery is the procedure of obtaining and reviewing all the evidence. As I was essentially indigent, and unable to work, my attorney was able to get the Court to agree to pay for an investigator and any experts we may need in our case, should it go to trial. I coughed up the money for Mr. Freeby out of some of my insurance proceeds. Many hours were spent over the next few months reviewing and poring over the alleged evidence against me. I obtained recordings of the radio transmissions between the police on scene and their supervisors, transcripts of the police reports, hospital records, lab tests, and so on.

Hung up in the cable barrier

In the recordings, the police and the dispatchers can be heard discussing the events of the crash and their opinions. One conversation was between a dispatcher and a detective supervisor thirty miles away in Olympia who had not been on scene. She asked "how bad is it if a motorcycle hits a cable barrier?" and he says that such a crash will usually result in death or severe injury. The talked and laughed (*yes, laughed*) over the alleged injuries we had suffered, then he said that speed was obviously a factor, probably alcohol too, and that they would "charge the motorcycle." In other words, without knowing any of the facts or being on scene, the State Patrol had already decided to charge me with being at fault in the crash. The "investigation" into my crash was a complete shit show… the State Patrol and Pierce County Prosecutor's office had decided ahead of time that the biker was at fault, and nothing was going to sway them from their preconceived ideas. The Trooper who first contacted me (*as I was lying in the grass, screaming in pain, with paramedics and bystanders all around*) even put in his report that the Audi driver and I were "playing cat and mouse" and therefore I was instigating a road rage incident. The truth is, I told the cop that "he was trying to play a cat and mouse type thing with us and I was trying to get away from him."

Despite numerous witness statements, the statements of the other riders who were with me, even the statement of my passenger did not mean anything. The deputy prosecutor, a spineless wimp named Tim Jones, even told my passenger Laura that if she didn't say what they wanted her to, that if she "stood up" for me, she would not see a dime of any of the insurance money. At that point, she refused to have any further discussion with them. Never mind the fact that the Prosecutor had no way to keep her from receiving her insurance money in the first place, but that didn't stop this little punk from trying to coerce her. Ah, yes, witness intimidation is alive and well in the Prosecutor's office. Their other tactic was, since she was my "victim" in the crash, the Prosecutors put a no-contact order in place between us (*as I mentioned earlier*), which meant we could have no contact at all: no notes, emails, letters, calls, or visits.

It's no secret that the Washington State Patrol had a vendetta against motorcyclists in general, and even had a "script" for dealing with motorcycles and motorcycle traffic stops. This bit of fantasy is called "Biker Basic 101" and was the standard procedure for years. Biker Basic 101 states: (*the spelling and grammar errors are verbatim*)
I. Bikers are dangerous
   1. Always use caution
   2. Bikers are attempting to gather intelligence too
      a. They just don't write the tickets

II. Identify the Violation
  1. In Washington, three main motorcycle violations
    a. RCW 46.37.530 – Helmet Violation
    b. RCW 46.37.537 – Exhaust
    c. RCW 46.61.611 – Handel bar height
    d. Other violations

III. Plan your stop
  1. Use caution
    a. Two officers is better than one
  2. You pick the place to make the stop
    a. Do not let the biker(s) control the stop
  3. The contact
    a. Be professional!

IV. Stopping a biker (one)
  1. If you can have two Troops have two
    a. Two against one is always nice, three against one is better
    b. Do not say it unless you plan on doing it
    c. If you can legally issue an infraction or citation do it
      d. If you can legally impound the motorcycle or book the biker do so. But make sure you do the same to other bikers, (be uniform and fair)
  2. Keep the Biker on the machine
    a. Kick stand up and machine off
    b. While inspecting the machine, kick stand up hands on the handle bars
    c. If other Troops (cops) are with you, get the Biker off the bike and to the rear or wherever you feel safest.
  3. Keep the hands on the handlebars
    a. No cigarettes
  4. If they have to get off the bike place them to the rear or front of the bike, or wherever you feel best
    a. Keep them on the bike when you can
  5. When you are with them take note of their patches, pins, tattoos, and anything else hanging on them
    a. Talk about their toys, (anything they have)
  6. Always check the numbers on the frame and the motor
    a. Know where the numbers are before doing it
      Go to bike shops
      Take classes on VIN
      Learn from those who know

       b. Do not look dumb, if you do not know, do not do it

V.   Talk to the bikers
    1. They are trying to get intelligence from you
    2. Make use of the time you have with them
       a. They have huge egos get them to brag
       b. Their bragging has value

       c. Talk to them about their patches
          Where they earned it
          How they earned it
          When they earned it
          What does the patch symbolize
    3. Take their pictures
       a. Get the patch and the bike at the same time
       b. Close up of their trinkets on the patch
       c. Do not voluntarily let them take group photos of you
          If you work bikes someone will get your picture

VI. Stopping multiple bikes (more than one)
    1. Get them stopped together
       a. Five will try to go five ways
       b. Stop who you want to stop, not who the Bikes want
          you to stop
    2. Have them stopped single file
       a. Keep the motors off and everyone on the bike
    3. Let them know you are doing business
       a. Be professional, they will respect that, to an extent
    4. You will probably have a loud mouth
       a. You maintain control, not the loud mouth
       b. Let them see the cover officers and you mean business
       c. If one obstructs let them know you will do business
       d. If you have a real problem talk to the Sergeant of Arms
          or President.
          Not best option – stay in control
       e. Have one contact officer
          Be efficient, one at a time and keep order
       f. Let the bikers know what you are doing
          Do not let the old ladies flirt – do business
          If they are too nice there is a reason
          Take notes with each bike
       g. Be professional
          Take the appropriate action

Cite them
Book, where you legally can – be professional
They will remember you
Tow wherever you legally can – be professional
 They will really remember you

5. Find the boss, President or whoever and let them know
   you are doing business – always be professional
   a. They will remember that
   b. I give them my card so they know me! I do business
      and the know that!
   c. Fair and honest - professional

In 2011, with help from Washington State ABATE, motorcycle profiling was *(allegedly)* outlawed with the passage of RCW 43.101.419, which states "(1) The criminal justice training commission shall ensure that issues related to motorcycle profiling are addressed in basic law enforcement training and offered to in-service law enforcement officers in conjunction with existing training regarding profiling.

(2) Local law enforcement agencies shall add a statement condemning motorcycle profiling to existing policies regarding profiling.

(3) For the purposes of this section, "motorcycle profiling" means the illegal use of the fact that a person rides a motorcycle or wears motorcycle-related paraphernalia as a factor in deciding to stop and question, take enforcement action, arrest, or search a person or vehicle with or without a legal basis under the United States Constitution or Washington state Constitution."

While the passage of the anti-profiling bill was a great step forward, there was no recourse built into it. In other words, it is illegal to profile a motorcyclist, but if they do, there is nothing anyone can do about it.

Believe me, I tried. The way that the Washington State Patrol handled the "investigation" was not only a joke, but in violation of their own standards. Remember, I said the first question they asked me was if I had been drinking. They never asked the driver of the Audi if he had been drinking, even though they knew by his own admission that he had been up at the casino watching a NASCAR race. Sure, buddy, have another diet coke. In addition, they never gave him a field sobriety test, never got him out of his car, never wrote him a ticket. They let him drive away, after trying to kill two people and trying to flee the scene. When presented with all this evidence, six lawyers I spoke with in an attempt to sue the State Patrol for improper investigation and profiling would not touch it. I even had a couple of friends who work in law enforcement tell me I should have sued the State.

Look, I have never bought into the whole ACAB *(All Cops Are Bastards)* line of thinking. Even with the way they treated me and some of my other friends, I know that the cops I dealt with are in the minority. I have friends who are in law enforcement *(I've even dated a couple!)* and have known many LE professionals over the years. That being said, I do have a sense of wariness when dealing with any law enforcement. I will be polite and respectful, but I will not say anything more than is absolutely necessary; especially after this experience. The time to argue with a cop is not on the side of the road, it is in a courtroom.

CHAPTER FIVE

Over the course of the next few months, I looked over hundreds of pages of police reports, witness interviews and court documents, listened to hours of recordings, spent hours with my attorney and attended nine court dates. Really great for a guy still trying to recover from a near-fatal crash. As the case went on, the Deputy Prosecutor and my attorney did battle...almost literally. There were arguments, heated discussions, and downright screaming matches between the two. An offer was made, a plea bargain, for me to plead guilty to "Reckless Endangerment," which took the Felony charge off the table in return for a gross misdemeanor. As he had an obligation to present the offer to me, Mr. Freeby did just that, but we rejected it right away. It was becoming apparent to the State that they really had no case against me, which only made the Deputy Prosecutor angrier. Eventually, on December 16, 2016, the charge against me was dismissed with prejudice by Pierce County Superior Court. As a result, the no-contact order was also dropped. "With prejudice" meant that they could never come back at a later date and try to charge me again for the same incident.

While the Prosecutor was trying to railroad me for something I did not do, the case against the Audi driver, Brien Applonie *(typically referred to as "shithead" in my life)*, was proceeding at a snail's pace. I made sure I attended every Court hearing, watching as Applonie sat in the courtroom smirking and laughing at the proceedings against him. After many delays, the trial was finally scheduled for April 7, 2017. I had received a telephone call from Mr. Jones approximately five weeks beforehand telling me they had reached a plea agreement with the defendant, and that he would plead guilty to one charge of Reckless Endangerment, and one charge of Reckless Driving. Mr. Jones' justification to me was that since Mr. Applonie was a nurse, pleading to less than felony charges would still enable him to practice his licensed profession, and therefore earn the money needed to pay court fines, court costs and restitution. In that telephone call, Mr. Jones also stated that Mr. Applonie "will serve jail time." I was happy, at the time, to hear that.

Off to jail!

The Prosecutor presented the case before the judge...a trained monkey could have done better. Mr. Jones, still upset by the fact that he could not sustain a charge against me, stood before the Court and acted more as a defense attorney than a Prosecutor. In fact, a number of the spectators in the courtroom said they thought Mr. Jones was indeed the defense attorney. Jones brought up that I had been drinking on the day of the crash *(remember, no evidence of that and a BAC of zero)*, and even mentioned that Applonie had no alcohol in his system at the time of the crash. How would he know? Again, the State Patrol never gave shithead a sobriety test or any other test to determine that. The jail time he referred to was a joke: a 364-day sentence *(the maximum allowed for one of the charges)* with 304 days of that sentence suspended, "home monitoring" of forty-six days, and actual incarceration of fourteen days. Mr. Jones even stated to the Court that Mr. Applonie had a "couple of infractions."

Applonie's driving record was littered with offenses: reckless driving in 2006, Improper Passing in 2011, 2nd Degree Negligent Driving *(which usually results from a plea deal on a DUI)* in 2011, Speeding 20+ mph over the limit in 2011, No insurance in 2012, speeding 10+ mph over the limit in 2012, Following too close in 2014, Speeding 10+ mph over the limit in 2014, and Speeding 11+ mph over the limit in 2016 *(only eleven days before he ran us off the road)*.

The Judge agreed with the Prosecution, and imposed the sentence as recommended, despite my objections, my passenger's objections, and our victim impact statements. As furious as I was, and as dumbfounded as the spectators in the courtroom were, it did feel good to watch Mr. Applonie handcuffed and taken out of the courtroom by a deputy to jail. But, as they say in the commercials; wait, there's more! Applonie's fourteen-day sentence was not really fourteen days. The defendant was released after ten days in jail. The reason given was that they automatically deducted 1/3 of the confinement. Their policy is in clear violation of Washington RCW 9.92.151, which stated that credits for early release due to "good behavior" shall not be credited to the offender in "advance of the offender actually earning the credits." Not only does the Pierce County Prosecutor's Office not follow the law, evidently neither does the Pierce County Jail.

In light of all this insanity on the part of the Prosecutor's office, I filed a complaint with the Washington State Bar Association due to the fact that Mr. Jones lied to the Court, presented facts that were designed to diminish or destroy my credibility, and lessen Applonie's responsibility for the crime. Of course, the Bar Association refused to even consider the complaint, much less impose sanctions against Mr. Jones. My attorneys later told me that a complaint against a Prosecutor almost never results in any disciplinary action whatsoever.

To make the understatement of the year, I was pissed.

CHAPTER SIX

One would think that, after the sentencing and his "jail term," the case would be over. Not so fast, grasshopper. Our education into the workings of the Pierce County Court system continued. The next few months were spent attempting to get restitution. Restitution is when someone causes damage and has to pay you back for the losses you incurred as a result of that damage. In my case, my losses were medical bills not covered by insurance, my lost wages, medical insurance costs *(since my employer at the time booted me off their plan)*, and costs for house cleaning, yard maintenance, and so on, as I could not do those things by myself. I tried to include my attorney's fees in the request, since the charges against me were dismissed and I would not have incurred those charges had Applonie not run me off the road.

As I expected, the Court didn't agree and threw out the attorney's fees right away. The remaining charges, however, were approved by the Court and awarded. My passenger, Laura, also presented her own restitution request which the Court approved as well. The restitution was added to Applonie's fines for court costs. In addition, should he not pay us the full amount awarded, the Court adds one percent interest per month on the unpaid balance. That interest, accrued monthly, is also awarded to us after the initial amount of restitution and court costs are paid in full.

We came to find out that the Court awards restitution, but cannot determine how much the defendant can or will pay each month, nor can they force him to pay any certain amount. As the Prosecutor told us, the Court has no jurisdiction over payment of restitution. Applonie filed an agreement with the Court saying he would pay no less than $25 per month. Not $25 per month to each of us, but $25 total. At that rate, it would take over 216 years to pay off his judgement, excluding the accrued interest.

I have always been taught to pay my bills. Quite a few years ago, a mistake on my federal taxes resulted in my owing the IRS $11,000, and not wanting to owe the government, I sold one of my Harleys to pay it. If I were ordered by the Court to pay over $65,000, I would figure out any way I could to come up with the money to get that monkey off my back. I did some research into Applonie's property and found he owns a house which had more than enough equity to pay this off and then some, merely by refinancing his house. In March of 2018, Laura and I wrote an offer to his attorney, offering to settle for a one-time payment of 75% of the original amount, thereby releasing him from further obligation…and getting him out of our lives. We gave them thirty days to respond. Not only that, but when the Court awarded restitution, they put a tax lien on his home, so he could not sell it without us getting our money…before his mortgage company got theirs!

No answer. It seems that Applonie would rather pay a pittance against the balance every month, while watching his balance due increase by roughly $800 per month because of the interest.

In late 2018, we sought out and hired an attorney who specializes in collections, in hopes of garnisheeing Applonie's wages. Because the writ of garnishment would be attached to a criminal case, there were endless hoops to jump through, the first of which was to get a Court hearing to request a subpoena to find out where Applonie worked. The problem was, the Court would not schedule a hearing, since it was indeed attached to a criminal case. The Court Clerk's office told our attorney that he would have to get the Prosecutor to agree to schedule a hearing. The good part of that was, since I raised hell with the Prosecutor's office regarding Mr. Jones' conduct and lack of competence in handling our case, we had a new deputy Prosecutor assigned, who was truly on our side.

Finally, we got our hearing. Evidently, Applonie had found out about our attempts to garnishee his wages, and he showed up in Court to fight it. A different Judge was assigned to this portion of our case, and she was having none of that. She granted us a subpoena to take to the State to find out where he worked. The Judge did put a restriction on the order, telling our attorney that he could not tell us where Applonie worked. I don't care where he works, I just want the money he owes us. The writ of garnishment was issued in December of 2019.

Yeah, I'm still waiting.

CHAPTER SEVEN

Meanwhile, I got all the usual questions a rider gets in the aftermath of a crash, including: "Are you going to quit riding?," or some variation of that. My answer was always the same, "you might as well ask me if I'm going to quit breathing. I've been riding since I was a kid, and I'm not stopping now." *(Yeah, my Mom was really happy about that.)* Riding is everything to me. It often doesn't matter where to, it's the fact that I am riding. The wind in my face and my knees in the breeze have always been therapeutic to me. So, there was never any doubt in my mind that I would ride again. The only issue I had was, I did not know if I would be riding on two wheels or three. But even in the rehab center, I was looking at bikes and deciding what to get next. I knew I wanted another Road King, and I wanted a newer one than the one I had, because Harley had made some changes starting in 2008: new frames, bigger fuel tank, a six-speed transmission, etc.

I found two bikes that caught my attention: one was a 2015 Harley Freewheeler, which is a stripped-down version of their Tri-Glide, a factory-built trike. I thought that if I had to be on three wheels, that was the way I was going to do it. But I was not ready to concede yet. I also saw a 2014 Road King at one of the dealers in Seattle. It was clad in a two-tone Sand Pearl/Canyon Brown Pearl: a gorgeous combination of light tan and root-beer brown. It had a few minor upgrades, and was the right price. I decided I needed to go look at this one, so Tammie and I headed up to the dealer. At this point, I still was unable to put any weight on my left hand or my left leg, so I was in a boot cast and hobbling around on a walker. We went in to the showroom where the bike was sitting, and were quickly approached by a salesman. We discussed the bike, I looked it over as best I could, then turned to him completely straight-faced and asked if I could take it for a ride. The look on his face was priceless…his jaw dropped, he looked me up and down, and stumbled all over himself trying to answer me. I finally gave him a break and let him off the hook, but his reaction was worth the hour-long journey up there from my rehab center! They had had the bike in their inventory for about a month and he mentioned they could "probably" bargain a bit on the price. I decided that was going to be my new bike. We went back home and I waited for my insurance payout from the old bike to show up. I knew it would not be long, the insurance rep had told me that the check was in the mail. About a week later, the check showed up, and I called the dealer to tell them I wanted to come back and look it over once again. That's when I got the bad news: the bike had sold the day before. OK, back to the want ads.

I was not ready to give up on the two-wheelers just yet, and I located a 2011 Road King down in Vancouver, Washington. After talking to the salesman, I headed out for the two-hour drive to take a look in person. It was beautiful: Sedona Orange color, tons of upgrades, a 107- cubic inch motor, detachable tour pack, and more. The price was decent, and we came to an agreement. Now I had to figure out how to get it back home. My friend Wayde said he would ride it back for me, and the next weekend we headed back down to Vancouver to pick it up. We did all the paperwork, and Wayde suited up and headed for home…well, not "home," but to my friend's motorcycle shop. I figured that since I still was unable to ride, I would have Jeremy and Jessica at Urban Custom Bikes fix it up into "my" bike. I had them put taller bars on it, change the exhaust, add cruise control *(hey, shut up…I love my cruise control!)* and other items. Every week or so, I would go in and check on the progress, but more importantly, I would try to squeeze the clutch lever. At first, I could barely move the lever at all, but as my wrist healed, and with the help of physical therapy, it got easier to pull that lever. After about six weeks I could squeeze and hold the clutch lever in, and told Jessica to get the bike finished up, I was ready.

It took another two weeks or so for them to complete everything I wanted, and I picked up my new ride. The seven-mile ride home was a bit nerve-wracking. Over the next few weeks, however, I got more and more comfortable on the bike, until one day when I ventured out on the freeway. As I merged into traffic, I became aware that I was tensing up and starting to breathe harder. I was hyper-aware of EVERYTHING around me, and it was not a good feeling, I got off the freeway at the next exit.

The "new" bike: 2011 Road King

A lot of people will say that riding a motorcycle causes one to be hyper-aware and super vigilant in traffic. I've been riding since I was seventeen years old, and the physical act of riding is second nature to me. The danger, which fortunately I was able to recognize, was that such acute awareness can rob you of your attention to the point where you won't see the next problem coming...until it's too late. Such a state of mind can cause overreactions: over-correcting, harder than required braking, or simply making the wrong decision at the wrong time. Not only that, but I was still trying to adjust to the way my brain was working after the injury, and learning how to process critical information as needed.

It took a while, but after a few weeks of riding local backroads, secondary highways, and in city traffic, I tried again. The vigilance was still there, but not to the point where it was debilitating. I caught myself overreacting a couple of times when a cager changed lanes suddenly or someone came up quickly behind me, but overall, I rode the thirty miles or so to Olympia with no problem. I worked on re-acquiring my skills over the next couple of months or so, and decided I could not stand it any longer: I needed a road trip.

I live for road trips. In the summer I am usually away from home more than not. There is an adventure, a peacefulness, a cleansing that happens when I am on the road. And since the last road trip I took was almost a year before, I was itchy to get back out there. There was only one problem: I had no idea if I could do it. In my previous book, Life Behind Bars, I recounted how a brother and I took a cross-country road trip that spanned twenty-seven states, one Canadian province, and a little over six weeks. I would do it again in a heartbeat.

Since my crash, however, I had only been riding locally and day rides, trying to get a feel for the new bike and my abilities and limitations. You know; lunch here, a loop around the Hood Canal there, a run up to Snoqualmie Falls for the afternoon. I needed to get away from everything, and most everyone if I am going to be honest about it. So, I decided it was time to hit the road.

I loaded up the bike, planned a two-day route, and decided that I was heading out. Of course, I did make a disclaimer: I may be back in an hour, later that day, or the next day. Not knowing how long I could ride or how my pain levels were going to be, I promised a couple of friends that I would be in touch later in the day to report my progress… or lack thereof, as the case may be.

I headed out of Tacoma, opting to travel the backroads as much as possible, and made my way south towards Oregon. Cruising easily through small Washington cities such as Napavine, Winlock and Vader, I noticed one thing more than anything else: my pain level was not aggravated by the bike! Another revelation became evident as well, in that I had to stop much more often to stretch, walk around a bit and try to loosen things up. I took a short rest break at a picnic area along the Cowlitz River near the town of Castle Rock, then jumped onto I-5 for about 25 miles, which put me into Woodland, and the exit to State Highway 503.

Eastbound on this scenic route took me into the foothills of the Cascade Mountains around Mt. Saint Helens. I stopped at a little park on the shores of Lake Merwin for a snack, then headed up into the Gifford-Pinchot National Forest. This is a road made for riding: it meanders along Yale Lake and the Swift Reservoir up to a Visitor's Center. I took another rest stop at the Center before riding up Forest

Service Road 90 and Curly Creek Road. I came to an overlook with some killer views of Mt. Saint Helens and the surrounding forest, so I stopped again and grabbed some photos. A couple of other riders were there and we visited a bit before hitting the road once more. A few more turns and I made my way into the municipality of Carson.

Even though it was mid-afternoon at this point, I knew I should start looking for a place to stay the night. If I had been in "pre-crash" condition, I would have kept going, but I was learning to listen to what my body was telling me, because pushing myself like I always had would only lay me flat for a couple of days and potentially cause more damage. Not only that, but I was already tired from the ride.

I didn't really find anything in Carson, so I opted to ride down toward the Columbia River and check out a small riverfront town called Stevenson. Trying to stay on a budget of sorts, I found the rooms in Stevenson a bit too much for my blood, and I crossed the river on the Bridge of The Gods into Cascade Locks where I found my home for the night. The Bridge of The Gods Motel was fashioned like a log-built lodge, with parking right in front of the rooms, and extremely reasonable prices. Even better, it was within walking distance of a number of restaurants. I checked in, unpacked the bike, took a nice hot shower to loosen up my tight muscles, and headed off to find some dinner.

The next morning was sunny and warm as I headed west toward Portland. After a short cruise on I-84, I took the Dodson exit off the freeway to put me onto US Highway 30, the old Scenic Highway. Growing up in Portland, once I started riding motorcycles, the Scenic Highway was always one of my favorite roads *(and still is)*. Running mostly parallel to the freeway, the highway winds and twists along the craggy rock cliffs of the Columbia Gorge, with hundreds of waterfalls and hiking trails. I spent a good portion of the morning checking out the various waterfalls, eventually making my way to Multnomah Falls, arguably the crown jewel of the Gorge. The tallest waterfall in Oregon, Multnomah Falls tumbles over 600 feet in two tiers from Larch Mountain, and is the most-visited natural recreation site in the Pacific Northwest.

A lodge, viewing bridge and pathway were constructed in 1925 and were added to the National Register of Historic Places in 1981. Normally, in the summer, this place is crawling with people and parking is almost impossible to find. Since I was there on a weekday and early in the morning, there was only a minimal number of tourists. Heading westbound from the Falls, US-30 begins to climb and curve up and away from the Columbia River before leveling out at Crown Point. Another popular destination for tourists, Crown Point is home to Vista House, a building originally erected in 1917 to give travelers a rest stop in the Gorge *(long before the interstate was even a thought)*. It sits majestically atop an outcropping of basalt rock over 700 feet above the Columbia River. One of many scenic points along the Gorge, it offers stunning panoramic views of the river and surrounding landscape. Now an Oregon State Park, it was designated a National Natural Landmark in 1971. Leaving Crown Point, I rolled through the serene countryside and passed through the small towns of Springdale and Corbett before joining up with the Sandy River and the city of Troutdale. I reluctantly hit the freeway and crossed into Washington on I-5 to make my way back home to Tacoma.

Multnomah Falls, OR

I discovered a few things on this trip: one, that I can ride longer distances; two, that a ride that used to take three hours will now take me four or five; and finally, and maybe most importantly of all, I no longer have to worry about the clock. I know I never really did, but my mindset has changed to the point where I can take as long as I want to go whatever distance I want. There is a freedom in that. My personality is such that I get focused on something and I go balls out to get there, but now I am content to take my time. Doing 500 miles in a single day is gone, my days are planned out for more like 250 or 300 miles. And that's just fine…. the whole "stop and smell the roses" thing.

Near Crown Point, OR

Over the next few months, I settled in to what would be my new routine. Since I could no longer work, I focused on my continued recovery and therapy. It soon became evident that I needed to make some drastic changes. The wet, grey weather of the Pacific Northwest was wreaking havoc with my pain levels, and I was quickly discovering that my disability income was not quite enough to support myself. I began looking for a new place to call home, and although I had been considering this possibility for a few years, now having a good paying job was no longer an issue.

My jobs over the past few years had been pretty physical, and because of my back injury I could no longer do those types of jobs. In addition, as I was *(and am)* reliant on pain medication to manage my pain levels, I would fail any drug test prospective employers want to give me. Not only that, I was experiencing bouts with debilitating pain, to the point where I was quite literally unable to do anything for a day or two, depending on the pain. The doctors have these little charts that ask you to rate your pain from 0-10, and even to this day, my "normal" pain level hovers around a six. Those bad days were when the level would shoot up to an eight or nine, and I'd spend most of the day on the couch or a recliner. As if that were not bad enough, about once every couple of weeks I would get hit with fatigue: I could sleep most of the night, but still be dead tired all day and take a number of naps. During this period of my recovery, the elevated pain days would happen about once a week, the fatigue would occur once every two to three weeks. No employer was going to give me a job with that much "sick" time off. To complete the picture, because of the Traumatic Brain Injury *(TBI)* from the crash, I was diagnosed with PTSD. My short-term memory was crap, my attention span was less than a hyperactive 6-year-old's, and even reading or writing was a monumental chore.

I began looking for other places to live, with better *(drier)* climates and a lower cost of living. I was looking at places all over the Western United States: Nevada, Oregon, Texas, New Mexico, and of course, Arizona. I did research, visited a few potential sites, and looked at as many variables as I could. As I eliminated one place after another, I was looking at either Southern Oregon or Arizona. During that summer, however, I visited some friends in the southern part of Idaho, and the more time I spent there, the more I liked it. I started looking into the area with regards to cost of living, medical care, climate and so on, and in December of 2017, I decided that was where I was going to move.

I moved to Idaho in April of 2018, and settled in. All the while, though, my wanderlust was kicking in and I wanted a road trip. My weekend trips and jaunts of a couple of days had been fine up to that point, but I wanted more. Not just a two- or three-day trip, but a major trip spanning numerous states. My friend Mike and I talked about it, and I asked if he wanted to come along for the trip. He agreed without much hesitation at all. Mike and I have traveled together on countless occasions, including my six-week, cross-country trip in 2011. We each know how the other rides, and our method of traveling is very similar. I had been playing with an idea for a road trip for quite a while, and during my downtime recovering, I was constantly looking at maps, playing with Google Maps, and picking out places I had not yet visited.

CHAPTER EIGHT

Music has always played a huge part in my life. There's a saying that "four wheels move the body; two wheels move the soul." I know for a fact that is true, but I also believe music comes from, and speaks to, our soul. I decided the basis for my road trip was from a song called "Willin'," originally recorded by Little Feat in 1971. A song about a trucker, the lyrics talk about traveling back roads and hauling contraband; but the lyrics that hooked me were "I've been from Tucson to Tucumcari, Tehachapi to Tonopah..." That sounded like a great road trip! I had previously been to Tonopah, Nevada and swore to myself I would never go back there again. As luck would have it, I discovered a Tonopah in Arizona, and added it to the route.

Mike and I planned the trip for June of 2018, with our first leg of the trip taking us to Reno, where we spent some time visiting my daughter and son-in-law. From there we went toward Tehachapi, California on US-93. The ride on the Eastern Sierra Scenic Byway through Inyo National Forest was relaxing and easy, with scenic views from the numerous outlooks we passed, and the further south we went, the hotter it got. Once south of Bishop, we skirted between Yosemite and Death Valley National Parks in 100+ degree weather. Even though we were cruising through the desert, the Sierra Nevada Mountains towered on the horizon, and their snow-capped peaks shone bright against the cloudless azure sky. A few stops for gas and to refill our water bottles allowed us to stretch and loosen up, and a stop in Lone Pine called for a cold beer to wash the dust out of our throats. Our original destination was Tehachapi, about 135 miles from Lone Pine; and over 350 miles from our starting point that morning. I knew that I was pushing it going that many miles in one day, but being that it had been an easy ride so far, I was hoping I would not be overdoing it. We sailed smoothly once again on US-93 until a hamlet called Indian Wells, where we turned onto Highway 14 for the last seventy miles or so into Tehachapi.

Mike & I; Lone Pine, CA

Then the wind showed up. Fully open in the Mojave Desert, the cross-wind came at us like a scirocco, pushing us all over the road and blasting us with gusts of sand and dirt. Occasionally we got some relief from the small hills that rose out of the desert, only to be nailed once again when we got into the open. We made a command decision to stop at the next town and try to find a place there, then go visit Tehachapi in the morning, hopefully when the wind would be gone. Tired, sore and dirty, we rode into the small community of Mojave.

Mojave seemingly exists to support the surrounding facilities of Edwards Air Force Base and Naval Air Weapons Station China Lake, as well as The Mojave Air and Space port and numerous aerospace companies. We found a motel, got checked in and unpacked the bikes, washed the grime and dirt off, and went looking for food. Mojave did not have much to offer in the way of food, other than fast food joints. After being on the road for 300-plus miles, we wanted more than just a McBurger and fries…unfortunately, that meant our choice was limited to one place: Denny's. Oh, well, at least they served beer. Playing it safe, I ordered a club sandwich *(hard to screw one of those up)* and Mike had a BLT. The wind was still raging as we walked the block back to our motel, and we prayed it would ease up before morning.

After loading our bikes the next morning, I discovered my shift lever had come loose and required a bit of minor surgery to get it back in place. This is a common issue with Harley shift linkages, and it was an easy task to tighten the bolts. A few minutes later, we headed west on Highway 58 for Tehachapi, and thankfully the wind had lessened to just a breeze. We got into town and found what we were looking for: the ubiquitous "welcome to…" sign. The one we found was on the edge of an industrial/residential area, and being early in the morning, there was not a lot of traffic. We parked the bikes in front of the sign, got our pictures, and saddled up. Although the morning was cool and dry, we were headed for Joshua Tree National Park and eventually to Blythe, our next stop for the night. We knew the heat was going to climb into triple-digits but we hoped the desert winds would hold off.

Straddling the Mojave and Colorado Deserts, Joshua Tree is named for the spiky, hearty trees that dot the landscape. Well adapted to the harsh climate, a Joshua Tree will typically grow an average of three inches per year for its first ten years, when growth slows to about half that. Joshua Tree National Park comprises an area larger than the state of Rhode Island, and is home to various scrub pines and bushes, rocks and dunes. The southeastern side of the park borders the Coachella Valley. Originally named a National Monument in 1936, the area encompassed about 825,000 acres. In order to open the land to more mining, the park lost about 290,000 acres in 1950. The Desert Protection Act of 1994 reclassified the area as a National Park and added 234,000 acres. Another 4500 acres was added in 2019, so that the park now encompasses over 773,000 acres.

Our plan was to ride through the park and stop at various scenic pullouts, while making our way down to Interstate 10 for the final 75-mile blast into Blythe for the night. Roads throughout the park are not well marked, and neither Mike nor I are blessed with a keen sense of direction. After cruising through the park in temperatures that

Hell would find cruel, I had a gut feeling we were headed the wrong way. We had passed an intersection about a mile previous, and so we stopped at one of the turnouts to check the map. The mercury had risen steadily since leaving Tehachapi, and when I put my kickstand down to get off the bike, it sunk into the now semi-molten asphalt! A quick check of the map confirmed that we had, indeed, missed a turn, and we headed back.

During the hour and a half or so we spent in the park, we saw a total of three other vehicles, normally what I would consider a blessing. The heat, however, was becoming absolutely oppressive, and we were actually looking forward to hitting the superslab of the interstate to get the wind in our faces. Our hopes were soon dashed to pieces as we ramped up the speed to 75 on the freeway… it was like riding into a furnace. Cool air was nowhere to be found, and we stopped numerous times to wet our bandannas and face masks. Getting into Blythe we found a motel at a decent price, got into our room, and cranked the air conditioner up to "blizzard." The motel had a pool and I went out for a swim to cool off. By now it was late afternoon and the temperature had climbed to a skin-melting 106 degrees. A few drinks and a couple of hours in the air conditioning began to make us feel more alive, and we decided to find some food. We went exploring, and found a small barbecue place called Rebel BBQ that we thought we would try out. Despite looking like it was a converted gas station, it was a great choice: the food was fresh, flavorful, and there was plenty of it! It was even better than some of the barbecue we had encountered in the Midwest.

CHAPTER NINE

The next morning, we headed off into the desert once again toward Tucson, and even though we had to ride a good chunk of the way on the Interstate, there was almost no traffic. We made a quick stop in Tonopah for a rest and to refill our water, then jumped back onto the freeway until we came to the junction with Highway 85 and headed south. Freeways to me are a necessary evil, and the more I can avoid them, the better. Anytime we could take a back road or secondary highway, we did. It was a short respite, only about forty miles or so, until we joined I-8 for the run into Tucson…but that forty miles allowed us to stay away from the madness in and around Phoenix. We found a nice little motel in Tucson, comfortable and clean and not too far off the freeway. Our next planned stop was in Las Cruces, New Mexico, but we took a small detour into Tombstone the next morning. Unfortunately, we were there way too early for any of the shows or events that take place, but we did find a great little place called the OK Café for breakfast. The weather gods were saying the temperatures were going to be pushing triple-digits once again *(hey, it was July, after all!)* so we wanted to get as far as we could before the asphalt began to melt. Rather than jump back onto the superslab, however, we headed out of Tombstone toward Mexico on Arizona Highway 80, through Pirtleville, which is a mere one and a half miles or so from the border, and home to about 1,500 people plus a Wal-Mart Supercenter. Arizona 80 became New Mexico 80 as we crossed the state line and rejoined I-10 eastbound into Las Cruces.

I'll tell ya, there is a whole lot of nothin' on that stretch of road! The thing we did see the most, once we hit New Mexico, were signs warning us of sand storms and telling us what to do in the event of one. Other cars and trucks were sparse as we rolled along the superslab, and it wasn't long before we were looking for a place to stop and grab a nice, frosty adult beverage. We stopped for gas in Deming, and looked for a bar or something where we could get out of the sun for a bit, but most everything was closed, as we were cruising through on a Sunday. Mike and I decided to scrap the idea of a frosty brew and blasted down the Interstate once more into Las Cruces. I had booked us into an old motor-court style motel called the Century 21 Motel. Reasonably priced and clean as a whistle, it looked like something straight out of 1957. The bikes were unloaded, the air conditioner was turned up to "igloo" and we mixed a drink to toast the day's ride. Las Cruces has a Harley dealer, so we called to see if they were open, and off we went. Mike is a big fan of his GPS, and he plugged the destination into his unit and we hit the road.

Arizona-New Mexico State Line

That damn thing took us everywhere but the quickest route to the dealer. Through neighborhoods, business districts, and side streets. And then, the sand storm hit. Remember, it was about 100 degrees out, so we were riding in jeans and t-shirts, and all of a sudden, we hear a noise… at first, I thought it was a train coming from the rumble it made. Then the cars in front of us began to pull over. The wind picked up a little, then a lot and the sand hit us full force from the side. We had pulled over to the curb and were literally laying on our gas tanks, certain that the torrent of sand, dirt, and trash was sandblasting the paint clean off the bikes. Damn, that shit hurt! It lasted maybe all of thirty seconds *(it seemed a LOT longer)*, and all was quiet once more. We made our way to the Harley shop, got our souvenirs and checked the bikes out. I also looked at a city map for a more direct route back to our motel and found one that was considerably shorter. What took us thirty-five minutes to get there using Mike's built-in GPS on his bike, took us ten minutes to get back. By the time we got back to the motel, we were done being in the saddle, but restaurants near our place were not plentiful: A McDonald's, a KFC, and a Dairy Queen. Thankfully, there was a Pizza Hut that delivered…pizza and drinks were the order of the night.

When I was planning this trip, based on the song, I knew that Tucumcari, NM was on the list, and we were headed that way. What I discovered was that Carlsbad Caverns was in New Mexico. Oh sure, go ahead and laugh, but I suck at geography, and living my entire life in the Northwest corner of the country, I had heard about Carlsbad, California for years. It seemed a natural assumption that Carlsbad Caverns were in Carlsbad, California. Ah, but not so… Carlsbad Caverns are in New Mexico! Not only that, but Carlsbad was not far from Roswell, and on the way to Tehachapi. Well, shit, we might as well go take a look. Looking at a map, I could have routed us through the White Sands National Park and Alamogordo, but opted to head a bit further south and into the northern tip of Texas…mainly because I had never ridden in Texas and I wanted to.

After a breakfast at Dunkin' Donuts *(they are non-existent in the northwest)*, we were off on I-10 toward the Texas state line. It wasn't long after we crossed into Texas that we noticed the road signs. Electronic reader-board type signs that were spaced every few miles, but there were usually two within a few hundred yards of each other. The first one we saw said "Look for Motorcycles," and the second one said, "Now Look Again." We saw numerous signs like this as we skirted around El Paso and began our climb into the mountains.

Our trip through the Lone Star state was only 150 miles long or so, but absolutely beautiful, especially toward the end when we skirted the edge of the Guadalupe Mountains National Park. The scenery here was unbelievable! The park is home not only to the highest mountain in Texas, Guadalupe Peak at 8,750-feet tall, but three of the other highest points in the state. Consisting primarily of limestone, the mountain range is also home to the world's most extensive fossil reef, according to the National Park Service.

We came back up into New Mexico and Carlsbad Caverns National Park. After a few obligatory photos at the sign announcing the entrance, we took the twisting, serpentine road up to the Visitor Center. It felt good to get into the Center and out of the 100+ degree heat, so we took our time wandering around inside. I bought a pass to enter the caverns, but because I still was unable to walk very far *(or very well, honestly)*, I opted to go down to the "Big Room" of the caverns. Mostly level and accessible even to those in wheelchairs, the Big Room offers a one-and-a-quarter mile pathway, with a shorter half-mile or so "shortcut" for those who can't or don't want to do the full trail. Mike had opted to stay above in the cafeteria while I went exploring.

The elevator descended about 750 feet in less than a minute and opened into the massive cavern. It has been said that the depth of the elevator shaft is one and a half times the height of the Washington Monument. I stepped out of the elevator into a fifty-six-degree, humid environment. All visitors are required to step onto something called a bio-cleaning mat, which removes potential traces of a fungus which causes White-Nose Syndrome. Thriving in cool and humid conditions, the fungus infects hibernating bats, and appears as a white fungus on their wings muzzle, and ears. Primarily transmitted from bat to bat, it can be spread by humans carrying the fungus on the gear and clothing.

This cave was truly immense! Sitting 750 feet below the visitor center, the cave is approximately eight acres in floor area, or just over 357,000 square feet. Will Rogers once said the Big Room is "the Grand Canyon with a roof over it." A lot of the more well-known features of Carlsbad Caverns are located in the Big Room, such as the Bottomless Pit, Painted Grotto, and Giant Dome. One formation, called the Sword of Damocles, hangs twenty-five feet from the top of the cave. The stalagmite formation known as the Great Dome is sixteen feet in diameter and rises sixty-two feet. As of 2016, the National Park Service completed an installation of all LED lighting in the cave.

I headed back up to meet up with Mike, after I had taken about 500 photos *(OK-- maybe I'm exaggerating, but not by much)*. We grabbed a quick snack, then went back to the sweltering heat outside. Our destination was Roswell, about 100 miles further north. We wanted to get there as quickly as we could, so with our water bottles filled and our bodies slathered with sunscreen, we blasted up US Highway 285 and made it into Roswell about mid-afternoon. Rolling through the main drag of the city, trying to get the lay of the land, our bikes were beginning to overheat. Rather than try to find a bar, we stopped at a local grocery store, picked up some food and drinks, then headed for our accommodations. I had decided to hang out in Roswell for a couple of days for a few reasons: I wanted to explore the area a bit, and I had made arrangements at Champion Harley-Davidson in Roswell for them to service our bikes. In addition to that, I knew I was going to need a day to not do much of anything, just take it easy. Not that I am lazy, but since I was still recovering from the injuries sustained in the crash, I would *(and still do)* get hit with those bouts of fatigue that lay me out flat. Not only will the fatigue creep up, but the pain gets so intense that I can't do much but sit or lay down. Sometime I can tell when those days are coming, but other times I get blind-sided by it. I had rented an Airbnb house that turned out to be just what we needed: quiet, comfortable, and about the same as what a motel would have cost.

Originally planning on two days in Roswell, I extended it to three because of a TV show I had seen. They were talking about a place called Ski Apache near Ruidoso, about 95 miles away. I know, we were there in July, it was over 100 degrees out, and we were riding to a ski area. But there was an ulterior motive: The Wind Rider Zip Tour.

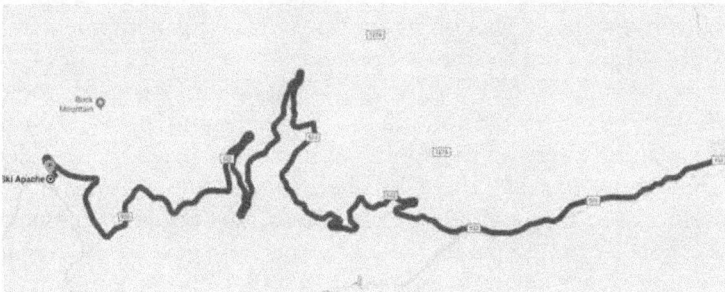

Road to Ski Apache

A little background is in order here. Ski Apache sits at about 9,600 feet elevation in the Sierra Blanca Mountains. It was opened as the Sierra Blanca Ski Resort in 1961, and is the southernmost ski area in the United States. Over 25,000 skiers visited the resort in its second season, and in 1963 ownership and operation of the area was turned over to the Mescalero Apache Tribe. In 1984 the name was changed to Ski Apache. The geographical location of the resort reportedly provides the area with the best skiing weather in North America, getting over fifteen feet of snow per year. Elevation at the top is 11,500 feet above sea level. As I said, we were not there to ski, we were there for the zip tour. Due to my injuries and limitations, I was not sure if I could do the zipline, but Mike had sworn he was going to go. After all, this is a guy who bungee jumped off the Stratosphere in Las Vegas on his 70th birthday!

We rode out of Ruidoso *(elevation 6,900)* after topping off the gas tanks and headed the fifteen miles up the mountain. County Road 532 is the name of the snaking, twisting, hairpin-laced ribbon that worked our riding skills to no end. Thankfully, we saw no other vehicles going up, and only about five coming down, because we barely got out of second gear the entire ride up the mountain. The Welcome Center *(sounds fancier than it is)* greeted us under a sapphire blue sky and no clouds, as well as a welcome 78-degrees. Once I saw how the rigging was for the zip runs, I signed up as well. The harness was sturdy and almost like sitting, so no undue pressure was put on my back. Two guys, Will and Dave, were assigned to us as our guides. Not only did they explain about the rules and regulations for the tour, but they gave us a little factual information as well. The Zip Tour starts out at 11,500 feet above sea level, which makes it the highest zip line in the world. At 8,890 feet long, it is also the fifth longest. We harnessed up, took a trial run on a small section of zip line outside the equipment shack so we could get a feel for the equipment, then boarded a tramway that took us about 2,000 feet further up the mountain. An ATV took us the rest of the way to the summit. At the beginning point, Dave and Will explained where we were going: Will pointed to a small spot down the mountain and said, "there." "There" was a mile away! He hooked himself up and took off. Dave helped us all get hooked up, two at a time on lines running parallel to each other, and gave us the signal to release the brake. The mile-long journey took less than a minute, and what a rush! Even though we were well above any treetops, I found myself tucking my legs up as I sailed through the air. The harness had a brake that was applied to slow us down from our 65 miles per hour speed to make it into the landing platform. After everyone in our group had come in, we prepared for the next run… a 1,700-foot ride down to the next base. Due to the angle of the line, our speeds again pushed the 65 miles per hour mark and the ride lasted all of about thirty seconds. The third and final leg of the line was 1,900 feet and crossed over the parking lot. Not quite as steep as the first two sections, this run took us about 45 seconds or so. Not only were Dave and Will knowledgeable, they were funny, professional, and extremely attentive to the group. Dave mentioned that, in the time he had worked there, he had made 400 trips down the mountain! Rough job…

Suited up for the zip line

Out of our gear and back on the bikes, we headed down the mountain into Ruidoso for a well-deserved beer and a great steak dinner. By the time we got back to our place in Roswell, that 78 degrees had long disappeared, and the temperature in town was pushing 104 degrees.

CHAPTER TEN

It was a good thing I had extended our stay in Roswell by an extra day. Nine days into the trip, my back decided it had had enough, and the fatigue hit me like a ton of bricks. Mike and I spent the day lying around the house, watching TV, and doing pretty much nothing. I learned rather quickly that, when planning a long-distance trip such as this one, I needed to plan for at least a day of downtime. The problem is, I never know when I will need one. But more on that later.

After a much-needed day of relaxation, and with our bikes freshly serviced, we headed for our next stop: Tucumcari, New Mexico *(Kudos to the staff at Champion Harley-Davidson, they did a great job getting our bikes ready for the rest of the trip)*. We headed northeast out of Roswell on US-70 in the cool morning, turned north at Elida, and rolled north up to Tucumcari. There was really nothing exceptional or picturesque on this stretch of highway other than farmland and a few small towns, but I loved this ride! It was relaxing, easy riding, and solitary...in the 160 miles or so we rode, I think we saw less than fifty other vehicles. Now, a 160-mile day was not normal, as we typically planned for 300 miles or so, especially after a few days in one place and very little travel. But there were a couple of reasons for staying in this little town on Route 66: one, it was mentioned in the song; two, there really was not much beyond Tucumcari for lodging, and three, it was on Route 66!

Yes, Route 66, the Mother Road, threads right through the center of Tucumcari. Located at the crossroads of Route 66 and New Mexico Highway 209, with US-54, New Mexico 104, and Interstate 40 also intersecting the city, I figured it would be a cool place to stay. The motels were typically 50s kitsch, mostly inexpensive, and there should be a lot of history we could experience. I love small towns, and usually will plan my trips to pass through those more than bigger cities. I have seen some that were still thriving, some that were all but dead, and many that were in-between.

Unfortunately, Tucumcari, despite its proximity to various highways, was more on the dying side. With a population hovering right around 5,000, there were more empty and abandoned buildings than active businesses. It was puzzling, since it is on Route 66, but we came to find out that the Mother Road is no longer the great draw it used to be. Tucumcari was originally called Ragtown when it was founded in 1901 as a construction camp for the Chicago, Rock Island and Pacific Railroad. Because gunfights were so prevalent, the camp became known as Six Shooter Siding until 1908, when it was renamed Tucumcari, due to its proximity to Tucumcari Mountain. Numerous TV shows and movies have filmed in the area over the years, including the 1960's western Rawhide, the Clint Eastwood spaghetti western For A Few Dollars More, musician James Taylor's 1971 film Two-Lane Blacktop, 2015's Hell or High Water and the 2018 movie The Ballad of Lester Scruggs. Unfortunately, even the popularity of the area for Hollywood films has not saved the small city, and it felt like just another community on life-support. Even the Route 66 Museum was struggling, only open for about three days a week.

The Federal Aid Highway Act of 1956, a "National System of Interstate and Defense Highways" is, in my opinion, mostly to blame for most of the deterioration of the small towns along Route 66. The reasoning was to eliminate inefficient routes of travel, unsafe roads, traffic congestion, and other challenges. Considered the greatest public works project in US history, President Dwight D. Eisenhower thought it to be one of the most important achievements of his Presidency. It didn't happen overnight, however. In 1919, as a young military officer, Eisenhower took part in a convoy of eighty-one military vehicles that made a trip across the United States from Washington DC to San Francisco, California. The stated purpose of that excursion was to see how well a large military group could travel under potentially war-ravaged conditions: damaged tunnels, destroyed bridges, even disabled railroad routes. It took over sixty days to make the 3,250-mile journey. That experiment made an impression on the future President. He was also impressed by the efficiency of the German Autobahns during World War II, where he served as Supreme Allied Commander in Europe.

The interstate system planned for 41,000 miles of multi-lane asphalt with a projected cost of twenty-six billion dollars *(the equivalent of over $255 billion dollars today)*. A Federal gas tax would pay for 90%, the States were to make up the remaining 10%. The detailed design called for speeds of seventy miles per hour, lanes were to be twelve feet wide, shoulders had to be ten feet wide, grades were to be less than thirty percent, with a required clearance of fourteen feet for bridges. Intersections were not allowed, so off-ramp and on-ramp interchanges were designed so speed and ease of travel could be maintained. Our interstates now cover over 46,000 miles, and the longest interstate highway in the United States is I-90, beginning in Seattle, Washington and ending in Boston, Massachusetts; over 3,000 miles later.

With all the speed, efficiency, and engineering that came with the system, the downside was that cities and towns were butchered or abandoned. Interstate 40, in particular, has essentially wiped-out Route 66 in Arizona, New Mexico, and Texas. Once people and vehicles could speed along to their destinations, many of the small towns along the old Mother Road were decimated. Parts of the old Route 66 still exist, but the majority of the classic road was swallowed up by the interstate.

We rolled into Tucumcari and cruised through it to get our bearings. We found our motel, but since it was still early, just past noon, we decided that lunch and a cold beverage would be a good idea. We found a place called the Pow Wow Restaurant and rolled in. The bar, called the Lizard Lounge, was a good choice: the servers were friendly and attentive, the beer was cold, and the food was top-notch without the top-notch prices! After lunch we headed toward our chosen destination, the Motel Safari. Even though we were early for check-in, the owner obliged us and got us settled into our room. A typical 1950s style motor court motel *(my favorite)*, the inn was built using architecture typical in that time period: geometric designs, perforated metal cylinders with lights, and square holes in the cinder blocks. From its opening in 1959 through the mid-2000s, the motel saw numerous owners and began to fall into disrepair. In 2007, the place was once again sold and renovation began, merging modern amenities with the structure's original décor. The furniture is mostly all mid-century modern style, photos on the walls are reminiscent of Route 66's heyday, even the clock radio in the room is tuned to a 50's rock station! Murals, prevalent throughout the town, were painted on the outside, depicting Elvis Presley and his 1959 Cadillac and a 1950s Santa Fe Trailways bus. The current owner bought the motel in 2017 and added two additional guest rooms and a fire pit/patio area for guests to relax. Our room was next to a small carport area in which we could park our bikes. Of all the motels we visited on this trip, the Safari was by far the coolest, cleanest, and most comfortable.

The next morning, we hit up a small donut shop for a bite and hit the road, rolling up US-54 back into Texas. An easy jaunt through Dalhart and onto US-385 took us north until we hit the Oklahoma State Line about thirty miles later. Cruising through the Oklahoma panhandle brought us into a small farming town called Boise City. Another community suffering from decline, its population has steadily decreased to where there are reportedly only about 1,000 residents. Boise City is smack in the middle of the Dust Bowl of the 1930s, which decimated the township. During World War II, on July 5, 1943, a B-17 Flying Fortress on a training mission mistakenly bombed Boise City. According to subsequent investigations, at about 12:30 a.m., the pilots mistook the town square's lights as their target and released practice bombs. Due to the hour, no one was killed. In true Oklahoma fashion, on the 50th anniversary of the "attack," Boise City invited the B-17's crew back, but all members of the crew declined.

I had basically two reasons for taking this route: I had never been to Oklahoma and wanted to ride through it, even if only a slice of it; and that I now live near Boise, Idaho. In many of my rides, I always look for places with the same name as other places I have ridden, so this was added to my list.

Mike and I decided to stop for a bite *(a donut only lasts so long)*, and we found a little café across from the high school. The Blue Bonnet Café sits in the middle of a gravel parking lot and is one of those little hometown cafes you wish every town had. We parked out front amid a sea of pickup trucks and SUVs, and found a table inside. While we were eating our burgers, we noticed a Sheriff's vehicle pull up out front, and the guy who stepped out of it could not have been more fitting if he had come from central casting: tall, lanky, wearing Wranglers, cowboy boots, a tan uniform shirt, a revolver hanging from his hip, and a Stetson cowboy hat. When he walked in, he took a quick look around the room, and was greeted at the counter *(by name)* and picked up his lunch. Reminded me of the sheriff in the "Longmire" TV series.

CHAPTER ELEVEN

Our next port for the night was about a hundred miles further north, in Lamar, Colorado. Surrounded by tiny farming communities, Lamar is what I call a big small town. The population is only about 7,600 people, which technically makes it a "city," but because it is the county seat, and the most populous community in the county, it has most of the amenities you would expect in a bigger municipality. Founded in 1886, it was named after the US Secretary of the Interior at the time, Lucius Lamar. The town was also affected by the Dust Bowl and is located on US-50.

Mike and I had been to Lamar previously, on our cross-country trip seven years prior. Due to a minor part failure on Mike's bike, we had stopped in Lamar to effect repairs in an auto parts store parking lot. As we were working on the bike, I noticed a small motel across the street, with a sign out front that said, "American Owner." That was intriguing. Just as we were finishing our road surgery, I saw a red Ford pickup pull into the lot, and in the back of the truck was another reader board-type sign: "Holiday Motel. American Owned." We got the tools put away and I told Mike I had to go check it out. I trotted across the highway and went into the office. The motel office consisted of a small seating area and a counter, and directly behind that was a small living room, where a man and woman sat watching TV. I asked if he was "the American Owner" as he walked up to the counter. He said he was, and that he had owned the place for about seven years, having bought it when he was 77 years old. He told us that, in a town with roughly ten hotels/motels in it, his was the only one owned by an American. Being that it was only ten o'clock in the morning, we couldn't stay there, but he even took the time to show us some of the rooms, starting at $37 per night. I promised him that if we ever came back through Lamar, I would stay in his motel.

A promise made; a promise kept

So, here we were, seven years later, checking into the Holiday Motel. Unfortunately, that sweet old man had passed away a few years ago, and the motel was now run by his family. But a promise is a promise, and we got into a clean, spacious, comfortable room for sixty bucks. We were feeling adventurous, and after making a stop at the liquor store to replenish our essential supplies, we decided to find a place for dinner. Both of us had the same idea…Chinese Food. Yeah, I know, we were in the middle of Colorado…not a place known for exotic cuisine. There was a place called the Green Garden just down the street, so we thought we would give it a try. Surprisingly, it was a great choice. The food was fresh and flavorful, and there was a lot of it!

After a great night's sleep, we continued our trek northward through Colorado. Even though we were on the eastern side of the Rockies in the prairies, Colorado is still one of my favorite states to ride in. We sailed north and a little bit west on US-287, then turned onto Highway 71. Wind farms, crops, open range, and oil wells were the scenery of the day. As we neared the intersection of Highway 71 and Interstate 76, we came into a little burg called Brush, and decided to stop for a cold beer. It didn't take long to ride through it, and we didn't see anything that looked like a bar or tavern. I stopped at a convenience store and asked someone if there was a place to get a cold drink, and she politely informed me that Brush was a dry town. All was not lost, however, as she said there was another city "a couple of miles that way," pointing west. "A couple of miles" turned out to be more like ten, but we rolled into Fort Morgan *(population 11,000-ish)* and found Cables Pub and Grill. Cold beer, friendly patrons, a well-stocked bar, and cute college-girl waitresses…good place for a break! There were a few other bikers hanging out at the bar and we had a good time discussing bikes, travel, beer, and girls.

We rolled out of Fort Morgan and headed north on Highway 71, where we came upon the Pawnee National Grasslands…a 193,000-acre parcel on the Great Plains. Extending to the Wyoming border, the area was used for some farming in the early 20th Century before the Dust Bowl devastated the area. Currently, the US Forest Service estimates there are over 60 active natural gas and oil wells located throughout the Grasslands.

We crossed into Nebraska under darkening skies and a threat of rain in the air. Our destination, Kimball, was only another twenty miles or so, and we got into town safe and dry. Our destination was a Days Inn Motel, and we got checked in with no problem. The wind was kicking up by this time, and the skies continued to get more ominous looking as night fell. Not wanting to wander too far from our motel, we had dinner at a Dairy Queen next door. Not one of those new, modern, parking lot Dairy Queens, this was a true throwback to the 60s era drive ups…and the milkshakes were top-notch! We were watching the weather closely, as reports were for heavy rain, hail, and strong winds. The next morning, we awoke to rain showers and more wind, and about ten in the morning all hell broke loose! The skies opened up with a vengeance, dumping over a half inch of rain in less than thirty minutes. The street outside the motel was a torrent of running water about six inches deep as the drains were pushed beyond capacity. In addition, the next leg of our trip was going to take us over the Rockies across the Great Divide at about 7,000 feet elevation. Weather forecasters were calling for high winds, severe hail and even the possibility of thunderstorms.

Old school Dairy Queen; Kimball, NE

Downpour!

Fortunately, Mike and I had made the command decision to stay another day and the motel manager even allowed us to park our bikes under cover. It was Sunday, and in the afternoon the clouds began to break up a bit, so we ventured out to explore the borough. The people at the motel said "downtown" was only a few blocks away, so we headed out on foot. It turned out to be more like a half-mile, which was okay, and we wandered a few of the side streets checking things out. Sadly, Kimball falls into the "dying small town" category, and even though a lot of the businesses were closed since it was a Sunday, we saw more "For Sale" and "For Lease" signs than active businesses. The good news was, we found a little dive bar called Beer and Loathing, about the only business in downtown that was open. Quirky, cozy, and friendly, the bar was opened in 2014 and has remained one of Kimball's resilient businesses. We had a great time visiting with the other patrons, the bartender, and having one of the best burgers we had eaten on this trip.

Still mindful of the weather, we decided to set out on the 320-mile trip to Rock Springs, Wyoming the next morning. The forecast had eased up a bit, still calling for rain and wind, but nothing too severe. Besides, we were not wanting to hole up another day in beautiful downtown Kimball, Nebraska. We packed the bikes, waterproofed our gear as best as possible, and suited up in our rain gear. This was not a leg of the trip to look forward to, not only because of the weather, but also because the ride was going to be completely on Interstate 80. It turned out that it was a better ride than anticipated, as we only got hit by rain a few times, and once we came down the western edge of the Great Divide the clouds began to break up and the temperature climbed about 15 degrees. We found a motel in Rock Springs, got unpacked and settled in, then hiked next door to a sports bar for dinner and well-deserved adult beverages.

A quick visit to Flaming Gorge Harley-Davidson in Green River started our day as we headed toward Pocatello, Idaho. Sticking with my preference of staying off the Interstates as much as possible, we rode up US-30 from Little America and through the small village of Kemmerer. Home to about 2,700 people, Kemmerer is where the JC Penney House and Museum is located. James Cash Penney, founder of the JC Penney department store chain, operated a butcher shop in Colorado before moving to Kemmerer in 1902. He was working for The Golden Rule Dry Goods store when they made him a partner and chose him to operate their new store in the Wyoming settlement. Kemmerer served the coal mines of the area, and Penney ran the store to provide goods for the residents and miners. Five years later, Penney bought out his partners and began to expand the stores into other areas of Wyoming, Idaho, and Utah, all while operating the "Mother Store" of the soon-to-be JC Penney chain. He changed the name of the stores from Golden Rule to JC Penney in 1913. In 1976, the house/museum was listed on the National Register of Historic Places and is a National Landmark.

We made a short stop at the Wyoming/Idaho border and continued into Pocatello to our motel. While not the nicest or best motel we had stayed at on this trip, it was comfortable and had a few other friendly residents that we partied with that night. Unfortunately, a bit too much of the adult beverage was consumed, and Mike was moving a little slow the next morning as we saddled up for the 250-mile ride home.

CHAPTER TWELVE

Once I was home, the bike was unpacked, and the laundry done. I went through my receipts and photos of the trip...all testament to the fact that I could still do long trips and multi-day rides. The difference was, where I used to be able to roll 400 or 500 miles in a day with no problem, now I was relegated to 250 or 300-mile days. I also learned that I needed to plan for downtime: a day where I just stay off the road, give my body time to rest and recover.

My next planned trip was to the western part of the Northwest in July. The route was simple: take US-20 across Oregon to Bend, where I was staying with my good friends Gary & Kelly for a couple of days, then continue on US-20, also called the Santiam Highway, over Santiam Pass and into Eugene. I had planned on staying the night there and catching a concert by country singer Trace Adkins at the Lane County Fair. From there, it was on to the coast for a couple of days of partying at Run 21.

Run 21 is touted as an old-school biker blast, and that year was held in Otis, Oregon, just inland from Lincoln City. The annual party has been in existence for twenty-one years, originally run by the Southeast Portland *(Oregon)* chapter of ABATE. I used to go every year for quite a few years before work and other issues got in the way.

I've been to many of the annual parties: Redwood Run, Sturgis, Doo-Wah-Diddy, and so on, but Run 21 was always my favorite! Local and regional bands show up to play, vendors are brought in from around Oregon and Washington, and of course bike games are part of the fun! I was going to meet up with a group from Washington and camp with them. These guys know how to camp: a generator, a huge BBQ, a large tent, enough food to feed a small country, and more importantly, great fellowship!

Having started riding again, Laura rode her 1200 Custom Sportster down from Tacoma to meet me in Eugene for the concert. The next morning, we rode over to the coast for the party. We got the tent set up, helped set up camp with the guys from Washington, and spent the next two days playing, exploring nearby Lincoln City, and discovering that I can no longer tent camp.

While the tent was big enough, and I had brought my inflatable airbed, I once again realized that with my injuries, humidity is not my friend. The temperatures during the day were mild enough, in the low to mid 70s, but at night it got very damp, which made it seem even colder. Being near the coast, the humidity hovered at 100% in the evening and overnight, and I could barely move each morning due to the pain and stiffness. That didn't stop us from having a blast the whole weekend, it just slowed us down a bit. On Sunday morning we broke camp and loaded up the bikes. Laura headed home and I headed back to Bend to hang out with Gary & Kelly for another day.

Since they had to work, I decided I was going to take a side trip, do the tourist thing and ride the Cascade Lakes Scenic Byway. One of Oregon's most popular drives, the route is only about 66 miles long, but travel brochures say it takes between three and five hours to complete. The reason for this is the number of lakes, trails, and scenic views along the way. I left the house about nine in the morning and headed south on US-95, then turned west and rode through a part of Bend to the beginning of the Cascade Lakes Highway. Closed between October and *(typically)* June, the road makes its way out of Bend's city limits and climbs into the Deschutes National Forest up to Mt. Bachelor. The views got amazingly more picturesque the closer I got to Mt. Bachelor, and as I passed the mountain, I caught magnificent views of the Three Sisters and Broken Top, well known landmarks in the Cascade Mountain Range of Central Oregon. The day was clear and mild, but as I climbed above the 6,000-foot elevation mark the temperature dropped.

One of the things I love most about riding in Central and Western Oregon is the forests: On a warm day, the verdant aroma of the pine trees perfumes the air with a musky, pungent, sweet smell that I cannot help but deeply inhale. Studies have shown that pine trees and their aroma are beneficial to one's health, increasing cancer-fighting proteins and virus-killing white blood cells, as well as decreasing stress hormones and inducing better sleep. After a day riding in the pines, I always sleep soundly.

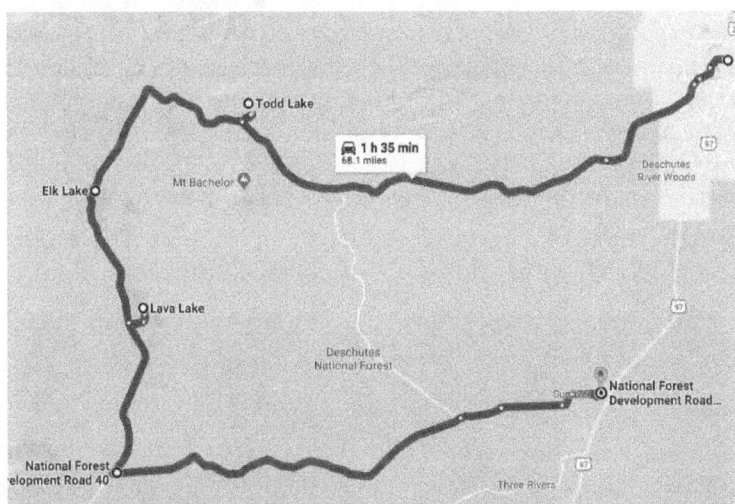

Cascade Lakes Scenic Byway

My first planned stop was Todd Lake, a forty-five-acre natural lake that I used to camp at when I was younger. The road into the parking area is gravel, but well-packed and only about a half-mile so even a street bike like mine had no problem. Even on a Monday, the parking lot was packed with hikers and fishermen. I found a spot for my scoot and walked the few hundred yards to the lake's edge. Just as pristine and clear as I remembered from all those years ago, the lake was quiet and still, with an occasional trout leaping out of the water. I found myself wishing I had brought a picnic lunch with me to enjoy at the lake's edge.

Back on the main highway, I headed west and came upon a small lake on the left just visible from the road. The color of the small body of water caught my eye, and I pulled off to a small turnout next to the water. Devil's Lake is bigger than it looks at first glance, encompassing about twenty acres, but is shallow with a maximum depth of only nine feet. This Devil's Lake *(there are two in Oregon)* was formed by a lava flow that piled a mass of volcanic rock at the lake's eastern end. Motorized craft are prohibited in these waters, which allows Devil's Lake to maintain its striking bright turquoise color. My next stop was Elk Lake, a considerable drop in elevation from Todd Lake and Devil's Lake, but also home to a sizable marina and resort. Over 400 acres in size, and reaching a depth of twelve feet, the lake sits at about 4,800 feet elevation. The resort is home to numerous campsites, cabins, a lodge, a restaurant, boat rentals, a marina, and swimming areas. I thought about having lunch on the deck of the lodge/restaurant, with its view of the lake and the forest beyond...until I saw the prices. Not wanting a huge meal, I looked at their appetizers and found nothing on it less than $13. Burgers, the primary feature of their menu, ran from $14 to $18.

Yeah, I know, I'm a cheapskate. I ordered an iced tea instead.

Todd Lake, OR

Further up the road about six miles, I saw a turnoff for Lava Lake Campground and Little Lava Lake. I left the highway and went a mile to the shore of Little Lava Lake. Separated from Lava Lake by volcanic rock, the "Little" lake is about 135 acres in size and is a popular spot for fishermen. The larger lake is a short jaunt up the road, and is home to a campground, small store, and boat rentals. Lava Lake covers an area of 368 acres and reaches over thirty feet in depth. I stopped at the store, bought myself a cold beer and went out on the dock to enjoy the sun and stillness of the water. Sitting on the dock, with my feet in the water, I could see the solidified volcanic flows along the edge of the lake as well as the tops of Broken Top and the South Sister. The water is clear enough to see the resident trout and chub swimming along.

It was time to start heading back, so I got my boots back on, fired up the bike and kicked it into gear. Running south for about seven miles, I turned onto Forest Service Road 40 for the ride back out toward US-97 and back up to Gary & Kelly's house. In all, the day racked up just over 100 miles…a perfect side trip!

CHAPTER THIRTEEN

In August I packed my scoot and saddled up for a ride to Victoria, BC, where I have family. Normally, I go as a "walk on" and leave my vehicle in Port Angeles, WA, but this time I took my trusty Road King across with me. On my way home, I stayed with some friends, Craig and Lori, in Washington, and arranged a day to get everyone together to hang out. There's nothing worse than having to run all over the place to see your old friends, so when I am in the Tacoma area, I make a plan for everyone to come to a designated place to visit. Lori was hosting a barbecue and we were having a great time hanging out, catching up, eating way too much…. you know, fun. In the middle of it, my phone rang, and I saw it was an Idaho number. Normally I don't answer calls from numbers I don't know, and since I was in the middle of a party, I let it go to voicemail.

Once I listened to the message, I called back right away. It was a guy from the Legacy Vets MC in Idaho calling to tell me I had won a prize from one of their raffles earlier in the summer. Every year, the local chapter holds a raffle in which they give away several prizes, with the grand prize being a new Harley-Davidson motorcycle. They sell tickets for $20 each, and only sell 2,000 tickets. I had bought two tickets at various times in June and July. The last prize of any consequence I had won was a new bicycle when I was twelve years old, so I never gave a thought that I would win, I just figured I was making a donation to a good cause.

Not so, however, because that phone call was telling me I had won the grand prize: a new 2018 Road King!

The conversation went something like this:

Legacy Vets MC guy: "Remember the raffle ticket you bought from us?"

Me: "Well, I bought two, but yeah."

Legacy Vets MC guy: "well, you won."

Me: "Cool! What did I win?"

Legacy Vets MC guy: 'Dude, you won the bike."

Me: "no shit???"

Legacy Vets MC guy: "no shit, man."

I told them I was traveling but would get in touch with them when I got home. A few weeks later, my buddy Mike and I hopped in his truck, rented a trailer from the local U-Haul place, and headed across the state to Chester's Harley-Davidson in Pocatello to pick up my new scoot. I was responsible for taxes, license, title, and all the necessary fees associated with a new vehicle, but the end result was that I got a brand-new Harley for less than $2,000.

I won it!

My 2011 Road King had served me well in the two years that I had it, but it never really "clicked" with me. The handling was drastically different than my beloved 2006 Road King, and it never seemed to have the power that my old bike had. I figured it was just that I was still getting back into the saddle, so to speak, of riding after the crash. Also, I had put 176,000 miles on my 2006, so that bike was like a part of me. I had put a lot of money into the 2011 King to make it fit my style, but although it was a really nice bike, it never quite felt like I was in love with it. My first thought upon winning the new bike was to sell it and pocket some easy cash. Then I realized, this is a brand-new bike with four miles on it…I would never be able to buy one if I had to. Based on that logic, and discovering that, even plain showroom stock, I was impressed with this new scoot: the power, the handling, and the ride itself was impressive. So, I made the decision to sell the 2011, and keep the 2018. Once I got the bike back home, I began to make a plan to personalize it: handlebars, exhaust, cosmetic modifications, and so on. When I worked at a Harley dealer, I used to tell people that the bike is only the down payment for all the things we do to them, and this was no exception. Of course, that also meant I had to sell my other bike.

The used motorcycle market had been soft for quite a few years, so I knew I was not going to recoup my money for the bike, plus by this time the "old" bike had about 35,000 miles on it. I listed the bike for sale on all the usual places: Craigslist, Cycle Trader, Facebook Marketplace, and so on. Not much was happening, I got a few calls and responses but nothing too credible, not to mention the usual scam artists wanting to pay me more for the bike and sending me a cashier's check to pay for it, since they were a missionary in Outer Southern Mongolian Zambesia and would have their agent pick the bike up. Yeah, sparky, I may have been born at night, but it wasn't last night.

I also decided to take one last road trip on the orange beast before parting ways, and I got out the maps once more. Figuring this was a great time to go explore my new home State, I planned a route east and north into the interior of Idaho, Montana, and over Lolo Pass back into Idaho… a nice, easy four-day loop, averaging 250 miles a day or so.

Toward the end of August, 2018, I saddled up and roared off into the sunset. Well, not really, it was more like roaring off into the desert, since it was morning, and I was headed east. I rolled down Interstate 84 for about forty miles before jumping on to US-20 near Mountain Home. Climbing and twisting toward the Sawtooth National Forest at the southern edge of the Soldier Mountain Game Preserve, this road is a dream for motorcycles. Mostly well preserved and sparsely used, the two-lane ribbon threads its way through the high desert and open rangeland for about 50 miles before straightening out and bearing due east to the junction with US-26 near Carey. The road becomes US-20/US-26/US-93 as it continues into the Craters of the Moon National Monument & Preserve. I remember always being intrigued by this place when I saw it on a map, and it has always been on my "to do travel" list.

Craters of the Moon National Monument was formed during several eruptive periods thousands of years ago. The area is comprised of numerous lava fields, and the geology has continued to experience "stretching" due to the unseen forces below the surface. The most recent evidence of this stretching occurred in 1983, when a rare earthquake shook the highest point in the state, Mount Borah, about seventy miles to the north. Measured at 6.8 on the Richter Scale, the earthquake added about one foot to the height of the mountain and caused the Lost River to drop by approximately eight feet. The US Geological Survey estimates that periods of eruptive activity have averaged 2,000 years between events. The Monument was established in May of 1924, and a presidential proclamation by then-President Bill Clinton in 2000 expanded the area of the monument. In 2002, the National Park Service parts of the monument were designated as the Craters of the Moon National Preserve. Spanning parts of five counties at an average 5,900 feet elevation, located halfway between Boise and Yellowstone National Park, the preserve is managed jointly by the Bureau of Land Management and the National Park Service. Three major lava fields and steep grasslands cover approximately 1,100 square miles, while the Monument itself covers over 53,000 acres. The three major lava fields all reside along the Great Rift of Idaho. The Rift is home to numerous open fissure cracks, including the deepest open rift in the world, plunging 800 feet deep. As part of the Apollo Space Program, NASA had astronauts perform a portion of their training at Craters of the Moon to search and collect rock samples, even though the 1969-1972 missions showed that the rugged landscape does not resemble the moon at all.

There is only one entrance to the Monument, at the northwest corner off Highway 93, which is the location of the Visitor's Center. Most of the massive preserve is undeveloped, with the only paved road running across the northern portion. Ranger-guided walks are available in the summer, but self-guided tours and displays are available year-round.

A quarter-mile long paved trail crosses the North Crater Lava Flow, the newest in the lava field, formed about 2,200 years ago. A longer, nearly two-mile trail is also available. In addition, there is a seven-mile loop road that provides chances to explore Craters of the Moon, with access to trails that take you over, under, and around some of the volcanic features. I spent quite a bit of time in the Visitor's Center and riding the Loop Drive, even taking the short hike to the Spatter Cones, which were created by amounts of lava as they erupted from a vent.

Once back out on the road, I headed east to the town of Arco, where I planned to stay the night. The hamlet was originally called Root Hog, and was located about eight miles from its current site at the crossroads of two major stagecoach lines. Town leaders applied to the US Post Office for the name of "Junction," but the Postmaster General thought the name was too common. It was instead named "Arco" in honor of Georg von Arco, a German engineer who was an inventor and pioneer of radio transmission and vacuum tubes. Arco moved to its present site in 1901. Less than 1,000 people call Arco home now, but its notoriety is rather historic. In 1955, Arco became the first community in the world to be lit solely by electricity generated by nuclear power. The event only lasted an hour or so, and was powered by the reactor at the nearby Idaho National Laboratory. More history was made on January 3, 1961 when the reactor was destroyed due to an operator maintenance error. The mistake caused a steam explosion which killed the three workers present. It remains the world's first and United States' only fatal reactor accident.

Arco has other fascinating history as well: The Number Hill and the "Submarine in the Desert." The Number Hill lies at the edge of the community, a rocky crag with numbers painted all over its face. The tradition of painting numbers on the hill began in 1920 when the graduating class of nearby Butte County High School painted the number 20 on the cliff as a symbol of their school spirit. Every year since, each graduating class has painted their year on the butte. Perhaps more bizarre, in the middle of a small park, lies the conning tower *(or "sail")* from the USS Hawkbill submarine *(SSN 666)*. Because of its hull number, it was often referred to as the "Devil Boat" as its hull number is considered the mark of the Beast in the book of Revelation. Chapter 13 of Revelation begins, "…I stood upon the sand of the sea, and saw a beast rise up out of the sea…" The Hawkbill was decommissioned in 2001, thirty years after the boat was initially commissioned. Town leaders convinced the Naval Historical Society to donate the sail to the town in recognition of Arco's contribution to the development of nuclear-powered submarines. Donations of time and money by Idaho's Tourism Office, the Department of Energy, Naval Reservists, and local citizens made the relocation of the conning tower possible. Even the truck drivers who hauled the massive structure to Arco did so for just the cost of their fuel. The submarine tower was hauled from Everett, Washington to Arco in the summer of 2003.

The Number Hill; Arco, ID

Today, Arco is yet another fading small town, but I found a really nice little motel to call home for the night. The room was small but clean and very cozy. A visit to a local café for dinner and the convenience store for a cold beer and I was set.

I headed out of Arco the next morning under clear sunny skies and turned north onto Idaho Highway 28, which threads its way between the Lemhi Range and the Beaverhead Mountains. For the next hundred miles or so, until I reached the junction with US-93, I saw a total of seven other vehicles on the road. I stopped in a tiny village called Leadore *(population 105)* because I saw the Silver Dollar Bar & Restaurant, and I was hungry. I'm often suspicious of tiny places like this because they have no competition and the food is often only passable, but rarely great. I was wrong. This place has great food, good prices, and I left knowing I would not need to eat again until dinner!

Heading north on US-93, I climbed into the Bitterroot National Forest and crossed the summit at Lost Trail Pass *(7,014 feet)*, a mere half mile from the Continental Divide. Entering Montana and dropping into the Bitterroot Valley, my map showed a few hot springs along the route, but they either did not exist anymore, or I was too directionally challenged to find them. Riding into the valley was a breathtaking experience; not because the road was challenging, but because the expanse of the valley, the surrounding lush and thriving forest, and the rugged Bitterroot Mountains combined to create a landscape unique to Montana. I descended about 3,200 feet into the small *(population 800)* community of Darby and began looking for a place to call home for the night. I passed a few motels and an RV park with little cottages for rent. They looked pretty nice, but above my budget so I kept rolling. I motored on up the highway another twenty-five miles or so, through Grantsdale and Hamilton into Corvallis, but still didn't see anything that tickled my fancy. I decided to take a break and popped into a place in Hamilton called Brewski's, a sports bar/casino-type of joint and had a beer. Just for the hell of it, I looked up the RV Park and called them to ask their rates. I should have stopped when I was there…they had a cabin available for $78 a night. I asked if they could hold it for me, as I was only fifteen miles away, and they said they would. I took my time finishing my beer and headed back to Darby.

Darby, MT

The Travellers Rest Cabins and RV Park was situated right on US-93, well laid out and looked super clean. The unit I was assigned to was a small log cabin with two queen beds, a sitting area with a table, a kitchen, and a full bathroom. A small patio area with chairs sat right outside. I unpacked the bike and walked a block or so to the local grocery store and picked up some necessities: some juice for breakfast, a couple of donuts, a couple of beers...yes, these are necessities! I've been pretty fortunate to be able to find great lodging at mostly reasonable prices in my travels, and the Travellers Rest ranks as one of the best ever. For dinner, I walked downtown and checked out some of the shops and found a bar called the Sawmill Saloon. The bartender was friendly, the burger was amazing, and the outlaw country they were playing over the speakers was perfectly appropriate for the little laid-back dive bar. The bartender informed me that the Paramount Network's TV show "Yellowstone" *(with Kevin Costner)* is partially filmed on the Chief Joseph Ranch about two miles south.

I really liked that little burg, one reason being that it is not another one of the typical dying communities. Darby appeared to be fully open for business. Since I was only passing through, however, the next morning I loaded the scoot and hit the road, heading north on US-93 toward Lolo Pass. It was a cold morning under a clear bright blue sky, with a bit of fog eerily hanging low on the fields. I made my way up to the town of Lolo, about fifty miles up the road. I gassed up at the junction of US-93 and US-12, then headed west toward Lolo Pass. But first, I planned a stop: the Lolo Hot Springs. As I pulled into the gravel parking lot, I noticed several dual-sport type bikes and parked next to them. As I was taking off my heated gear and chaps, a couple of guys came out to the bikes. They were from California, on their way back home after riding up to Glacier National Park. We talked a bit about our travels, they were kind enough to let me know about the road construction up on the Pass. As they got ready to leave, I grabbed my swimsuit and towel and went inside.

It turned out to be the perfect stop on a frosty cold morning in the mountains. The facility has an outdoor pool and an indoor mineral pool, with naturally occurring temperatures of about 103 degrees F. More than just the pools, the hot springs also has a frisbee golf course, casino, restaurant and lounge, RV Park, camping cabins and tent camping. Kayaking and rafting are available on the nearby Lochsa River. I paid my fee and got into the mineral pool, letting the water soak into my muscles and warm me up.

It had warmed up a little bit by the time I was ready to head out, and I rolled west toward the summit, about eight miles away. That's where I found the construction: road projects and rebuilding were taking place and much of the travel lane was reduced to well-packed gravel. I stopped at the summit for a bathroom break and pictures *(no, not of me in the bathroom)*. Lolo Pass is part of the Bitterroot Range and reaches an altitude of just over 5,200 feet on the border of Montana and Idaho, the highest point of the Lolo Trail. The trail was used by Lewis & Clark in 1805 on their expedition west and figured prominently in the Nez Pierce War of 1877. The highway, US-12, was completed in 1962, and in true Western fashion, the governors of Idaho and Montana dedicated the opening by cutting a cedar log with a two-man crosscut saw. I got back onto what was left of the road and began motoring down the hill into Kooskia, where I stopped and visited with some old friends who were building a house there.

I made my way out of Kooskia southbound on Idaho Highway 13 to Grangeville. My map had showed a few turns that would lead me through the fertile farmlands out to US-95, but in true rural backroads fashion, almost none of the intersections had street signs. I was left to my own sense of direction to find my way into Grangeville, a small farming community along US-95. The problem is, my sense of direction really sucks. So, being the guy who never gets lost, I did what I usually do: took the "scenic route." OK, I did resort to using my compass to make sure I was still headed either west or south, and I soon found myself rolling into Grangeville. US-95 took me south along the banks of the Salmon River into Riggins, the northwestern-most town in Idaho in the Mountain Time Zone. With only about 400 full-time residents, Riggins is a popular place in the summer for rafters, fishermen, hikers, and other outdoor enthusiasts. It also serves as a jumping off point for access to the Seven Devils Mountains and Hells Canyon. I got a room for the night at the Salmon River Motel and called it a day, 275 miles from my start in Darby. The next day was an easy 165-mile ride home, and I got the bike unloaded, cleaned up and back on the market for sale. It was a bittersweet feeling: the bike I had bought after my crash was going away. On the other hand, the new Road King sitting in the garage was also calling my name. I began riding it to get through the break-in period, all the while planning the modifications I was going to effect to make it "my" bike.

The Orange Beast finally sold, for much less than I wanted, but that's what happens in a soft used bike market, not to mention that I was selling at the end of the riding season. With my wish list complete, or mostly complete anyway, I loaded the new bike on a trailer and headed to my friends' shop in Lacey, Washington. Jeremy and Jessica at Dead Center Cycles have worked on my bikes for years, and I knew I could trust them to give me what I wanted. Over the next couple of months *(I was in no hurry)*, they tore down the new Road King and made it into something that was all mine.

Made some changes…

The last thing on the planet that I would have bought for myself is a black Harley, as damn near every other one you see is just that… ho-hum, another black Harley. Since the new bike is a stereotypical black hog, rather than chrome it out like I had done in the past, I opted instead to black it out. This was a big decision and a major departure for me: I am a self-admitted chrome whore. I love chrome. Shiny, bright, flashy, sexy chrome. On this scoot, however, a set of black sixteen-inch ape hanger handlebars and black controls were installed, black luggage rack and passenger backrest, and black engine guard were added. Then they disassembled the front end and powder coated the forks, nacelle, light housings, and center fuel tank console. Engine work included powder coating the rocker boxes, primary covers, and transmission housing covers. They added a Feuling .475 cam for performance, with a Bassani 2-into-1 exhaust, pushing the bike to a healthy 102 horsepower and 107-foot pounds of torque.

I got it back home and began to ride it locally in earnest. The more I ride this bike, the more I love it!

CHAPTER FOURTEEN

Spring was fast approaching, and I was looking at maps…again. In addition to exploring my local area, I was itching once more for a road trip. My road trip ideas come from many sources: books, TV shows, songs and song lyrics, and just about anything that catches my interest.

I was *(and am still)* a huge fan of the TV show "Longmire," about a county sheriff in Wyoming. I have all the books upon which the series is based, have met the author on a couple of occasions, and have seen all the episodes of the six-season program. The show became so popular that an event called Longmire Days was started in Buffalo, Wyoming. Buffalo is the model and serves as the setting for the stories' fictional town of Durant, Wyoming. Every year, the city of Buffalo hosts Longmire Days and the thousands of fans who descend on it to share their love of all things Longmire. Many of the stars of the show come in for the event, and the community of 5,000 people becomes a bustling hub of over 12,000 for a few days each summer. Author Craig Johnson lives near Buffalo, in a tiny bump in the road called Ucross. I decided my summer trip was going to be attending Longmire Days.

In typical fashion, however, I could not just plan a trip to go to a small burg in Wyoming and back…so I started playing with the maps.

I knew I was going to be in Buffalo or about four or five days, so the trip centered around that, but I figured I could throw in some other places I wanted to go as well. My trip plans are pretty well planned out because I am the type that tends to overthink everything, but they are also not written in stone. Planning is also important due to the residual effects of my crash. If I want to change it up when I am on the road, I do. My first "leg" of this journey was going to be to head south. Yeah, I know, I was headed south; Buffalo, Wyoming was north. But bear with me here.

Over the course of the next month or so, the excursion began to take shape. I was planning on leaving in July, and by June I had my route planned: The Grand Canyon, the Four Corners, Colorado's Million Dollar Highway, Longmire Days, Yellowstone National Park, and home. Almost as soon as I had my route planned, Laura asked if I wanted to join her at her son's wedding at the end of July in the uppermost part of Washington State, and she and I could ride back home afterward. So, out came the maps once more, and I added a few more stops to the trip. By now, it penciled out at just over three weeks on the road. Perfect!

After much planning, budgeting and preparation, my departure day was finally here. I headed out of town on Idaho Highway 45, crossed the Snake River and began rolling southeast on Highway 78 along the foothills of the Owyhee Mountains. This is a desolate road with very little traffic, slicing through the high desert landscape. Just before the hamlet of Grandview, the road passes through the southernmost end of the Morley Nelson Birds of Prey Wildlife Refuge.

Managed by the Bureau of Land Management, the refuge provides a home to the largest concentration of birds of prey in North America, with over 800 pairs of owls, falcons, hawks, and eagles mating and nesting each spring. The refuge spans just under 485,000 acres and covers portions of four counties. Originally designated as the Snake River Birds of Prey National Conservation Area (NCA) in 1993, the Omnibus Public Lands Protection Act of 2009 renamed the area in honor of Morley Nelson, a national raptor expert and a major force in creating the initial NCA. In addition to the raptor residents, the NCA is also home to the world's densest population of badgers and ground squirrels…good eating for the birds. Not only is the refuge home for wildlife, it also has historical significance: some of the best-preserved parts of the Oregon Trail are located within its boundaries, as well as three portions of an 1850s gold mining camp and some of the oldest Native American archaeological sites.

As I was riding this section of the highway, it began to twist and climb a bit toward Grandview, and as I rounded a curve, a Golden Eagle took flight from where he was perched atop a guardrail post... right in front of me. Scared the shit out of me! I barely had time to recognize an unfamiliar shape sitting on the post when he majestically spread his wings and launched, most likely frightened by the throaty rumble of my bike. Smaller than a Bald Eagle, the Golden Eagle is no less impressive: a wingspan of between six and eight feet, and up to three and a half feet in length. This is one gorgeous creature that definitely commands your attention!

My journey continued without incident another twenty-five miles or so to the town of Bruneau and the junction with Idaho Highway 51. I turned south and sailed effortlessly along the sparse desert landscape into Nevada, where the asphalt then becomes Nevada Highway 225. Continuing on through the Shoshone-Paiute Tribes' Duck Valley Reservation and the village of Owyhee, I made a quick gas stop and grabbed a snack. This stretch of road followed Machado Creek as I climbed into the Owyhee Mountains, crossing Wild Horse Reservoir, a 2,800-acre man-made lake created in 1937 by the construction of Wild Horse Dam. It was a nice treat to see the shimmering blue waters of such a large lake in the middle of the desert.

Highway 225 continued all the way into downtown Elko, a city of about 20,000 people along Interstate 80, first incorporated in 1917. I found a motel for the night called the Budget Inn and unloaded my scoot. After a quick shower to wash away the road grime and dust, I headed over to Gold Rush Harley-Davidson to check out the place and pick up a souvenir, since I had never been this way before. Gold Rush is a small dealership, but Chris, the manager, was very outgoing and we talked for about forty-five minutes about bikes, traveling, and many things Harley. For dinner, I headed back downtown to Stockman's Bar and Casino for a ten-dollar Prime Rib dinner. Nothing fancy, but the eight-ounce steak was perfectly cooked, the food was hot, and the service was great! Stockman's is featured prominently in an old Ian Tyson song and is host to the annual National Cowboy Poetry Gathering. Held every January for the past thirty-five years or so, it is a week-long celebration of the rural West spotlighting poetry, music, food, photography, and stories; and draws Western celebrities and musicians from all over the world. Since I had been in the saddle all day, I took a little walk around and stopped in at a cozy little bar where I had a beer while watching part of a baseball game, then went back to the motel for the night.

A quick breakfast at a fast food joint the next morning quieted my growling stomach and I headed out on a 300-mile journey further south into the desert. Forsaking the busier US-93, I opted to run the secondary road, Nevada Highway 228, through Ruby Valley, a picturesque basin of open range, cattle ranches, and alfalfa farmland that sits at about 6,000 feet in the Ruby Mountains. A five-mile stretch of road construction slowed me down a bit, as the road was undergoing seal-coating and loose gravel was everywhere. The nice part was, after that initial five miles or so, the road surface was brand new pavement and all mine...I did not see another vehicle for over an hour. The Shoshone Nation used to use Ruby Valley as a winter home since it was warmer overall than other nearby areas. In 1846, the infamous Donner Party traversed the southern portion of the valley on their way to the Overland Pass to cross the Ruby Mountains. A nice surprise along the route was the sight of the Ruby Lake National Wildlife Refuge, a wetland oasis of over 360,000 acres with an enormous lake stretching ten miles from shore to shore. At the southern end of the lake is the site of the former Fort Ruby, an outpost built in 1862 by the US Army in order to protect the Pony Express and overland coaches.

The road ended at US-50, "the Loneliest Road in America," which I had ridden in 2011. A left turn put me on track for the city of Ely, originally a stagecoach station and mining boom town. First established as a gold mining camp in 1878, it also served as a stagecoach station and Pony Express stop. The discovery of copper in 1906 caused a mining boom that saw the town grow, then go bust. Currently with a population estimated at 4,000 people, the town is a welcome sight to travelers on the desolate Highway 50 route. I topped off the gas tank and rode downtown, thinking I would pick up a quick snack for lunch, when I saw the Economy Drug & Old-Fashioned Fountain. Stepping into the cool store from the heat of the day, I spotted an old-fashioned soda fountain to my right, and ordered a root beer float. Just what I needed! The food looked really good too, but I was not that hungry and polished off the foamy confection in no time...tempted to order a second one!

On my way out of town, however, I decided a cold beer would be in order and I stopped at a little bar with a couple of other bikes out front. The bikes belonged to a couple traveling the American

West from 100 Mile House in Northern British Columbia, and we had a great time chatting and talking about the joys and pitfalls of motorcycle travel.

Refreshed and with a full tank of fuel, I motored down US-50 a short way before turning south on US-93. My destination was a town called Panaca, about 100 miles away. Skirting the eastern edge of the State, this is once again very isolated country, but surprisingly a very nice ride. As I neared a small borough called Pioche, I decided I needed to refill my water bottle and pulled in to a gas station/repair shop/convenience store. They didn't have a machine for fountain drinks, so I picked up a bottle of water from the cooler, and waited for a cashier or someone to come take my money. After about five minutes no one did, so I simply left some cash on the counter by the register and headed out.

Not far beyond Pioche, I came across Cathedral Gorge, a siltstone and shale canyon covering 1600 acres. In 1911, two teenaged boys from the area began to explore the nooks and crannies of the gulch, and built numerous ladders throughout the crevices and crawlways. The family was later instrumental in efforts to protect and preserve the area, leading to Cathedral Gorge being named a state park in 1935. Camping facilities and a stone water tower were erected by the Civilian Conservation Corps, as well as the open structure at the main observation point. The park now features a campground, ADA accessible sites, restrooms with showers, and a visitor center. The views at this place are amazing...like a miniature version of the Grand Canyon with multicolored stone and spires reaching to the sky from the desert floor.

I reached my destination for the night about five miles later, the "town" of Panaca. Towns in this part of Nevada are sparse, and motels even more rare, so I had booked a room at the Pine Tree Inn bed & breakfast before I left home. The B&B was located on a side street off the main road. My typical routine is to ride through a town to find out where the restaurants are, the bars, the stores, and so on to get a feel for the place. I stopped at a gas station at the junction of US-93 and Nevada Highway 319 to top off the tank, then headed east into ... town?

Panaca is not much of a city *(sorry, residents)*. With a population of reportedly 1,000 residents, you'd never know it: there is a post office, a high school, a middle school, a church, a fire department, and a small grocery store. Founded in the 1860s as a Mormon farming community, it is the oldest surviving town in Eastern Nevada, and

95

many of Panaca's residents are direct descendants of the original settlers. I was hoping for a quaint café or diner to get some dinner, but the only place I saw, other than the Shell station out on the highway, was a taco truck. So, I picked up a couple of beers from the store, ordered a burrito from the taco truck, and headed back to the B&B to have my dinner. I was the only person there at that point, so I sat on a nice, covered patio and kicked back. The room at the B&B was very comfortable and quiet, and being in the basement was nice and cool after riding in the near-triple digit heat of the day. Breakfast the next morning was typical B&B fare: eggs, fruit, pastries, pancakes. There were two other couples there that I didn't even know were staying there, that's how quiet this house was. One young couple, from central Oregon, was on their honeymoon and exploring the desert and mountains around the area in a lifted, beefed up Chevy Suburban that was clearly modified for off-road. They told me of their adventures exploring forgotten mines and ghost towns all over the West while I told them about my road trip.

Cathedral Gorge, NV

After breakfast I got the bike loaded back up and headed east out of Panaca on Highway 319. Twenty miles later I crossed into Utah, where the road changed to Utah Highway 56. This was going to be a long day, not only because of the estimated miles in the saddle, but also because I was going to the Grand Canyon.

I topped off the tank in Cedar City, then headed south on Interstate 15 for about twenty-three miles and took Highway 17 south to the small city of Hurricane. Even though there had been a pretty good chill in the air when I left Panaca, the sun was ramping up and the temperature was climbing. On the border of Utah and Arizona, at a place called Hildale, I topped off the gas tank once again, not knowing where the next gas station would be. I also took the opportunity to get out the sunscreen and to refill my water bottle.

I always carry an insulated water bottle with me on the road, ever since a trip into the Canadian Rockies years ago that left me severely dehydrated and sick. On that trip, a few of us had ridden from Calgary to Edmonton, a relatively short ride on a nice, cool, semi-cloudy day with temperatures in the mid-70s. I'm not sure why that particular day I got so dried out, but the next morning I woke up and thought I had the flu: chills, aches everywhere, what I thought was a fever, and so on. One of the people with me on the trip suggested that I may be dehydrated, and I began drinking water. The more I drank, the better I began to feel, and over the course of the day I must have ingested about three gallons of water. We promptly made a trip to the Harley dealer and bought a cup holder for my scoot, and I have had one on every bike since.

The nice thing is, when I am on the road, most of the quickie mart-gas stations and fast-food restaurants have fountain drinks, and I have almost never been turned down or charged for refilling my bottle with water. I always ask, and only on two occasions have they tried to charge me: once in Packwood, Washington *(they charged for the ice);* and McDermitt, Nevada *($1 to fill my bottle).*

Crossing into Arizona, I headed east on Highway 389 and then south onto US-89A through the Kaibab National Forest for the run to the Grand Canyon. I stooped at the LeFevre Overlook, a turnout at 6,700 feet elevation from which I could see the Grand Staircase National Monument in Utah, about twenty-five miles away. At one time, this area was reportedly the bottom of a shallow sea, and evidence of prehistoric aquatic life can be found all over the Kaibab Plateau. There is a short hike uphill from the parking area to the overlook point itself, but the climb is well worth it. From this height, I was able to see the "steps" of the plateau, caused by ancient geologic forces that lifted the entire mesa and slanted this portion of it on its edge. Looking across the vast landscape, I saw a small mountain that almost looked out of place in the panorama: Mollie's Nipple *(stop giggling).*

Mollie's Nipple is a unique landmark cone of sandstone that has been eroded into its current shape, rising 1,300 feet above the Colorado Plateau. I know, the reason I found this so interesting is not only because of the anomaly of a cone peak rising out of the plateau, but also because I'm mentally about fifteen years old and am fascinated by boobs and nipples. *(Hey, name five guys that aren't...)* I found out that Mollie's Nipple is the name of numerous peaks, a butte, a well and other geology in this area. Most, if not all, of these names can be traced back to John Kitchen, an early explorer and homesteader of Utah, who named them to commemorate one of his wife's nipples. I couldn't find much on John Kitchen, nor any photos, but Ol' Molly must have had a great rack!

Not just the name is story worthy, however, as the formation was well-known to the early explorers of the landscape, and because the indigenous people of the early West used the caves at the bottom of the "nipple" for cooking. The butte above was also used to send smoke signals to the hunting parties, since it could be seen for miles.

At Jacob Lake, the road branches off to Highway 67, also known as the Grand Canyon Highway, and runs due south for about forty miles to Grand Canyon National Park. Heavy gray rain clouds and thunderstorms were forming off in the distance as I rode this absolutely gorgeous thread of pavement through the stands of pine and aspen trees.

The Grand Canyon Highway was once a trail, then a Forest Service Road, before being paved in 1940 and designated a National Scenic Byway in 1998. Well-maintained and offering panoramic views of the surrounding area, this byway has everything from straightaways to lazy sweeping curves and tight turns. Turnouts are sparse along this stretch of pavement, but that doesn't mean it is any less picturesque. About halfway between the junction with Highway 89A and the North Rim Entrance to the Grand Canyon is the Kaibab Plateau High Point, a mere 9,200 feet above sea level. It appears imposing from a distance, but there are many ways to get to the summit via hiking, OHVs, and motorcycles. Hikers endure a 700-foot climb to the top, which encompasses a distance of about ten miles round-trip, and a time frame of about six hours.

CHAPTER FIFTEEN

Still heading south

I arrived at the entrance to Grand Canyon National Park, showed my pass and rode on in. The weather had cooled a bit from the 93 degrees when I crossed the Utah-Arizona state line to a much more comfortable 80 degrees at the Grand Canyon Lodge. There were a couple of reasons for the drop: first, the altitude had climbed to about 8,500 feet, but also because of the nearby thunderstorms rolling through the area. While the temperature may have dropped, the humidity had climbed significantly. Since I was there in the middle of summer, the place was jam packed with tourists from all over the world, but I was able to find a fairly safe parking spot for the bike and locked it up. I walked up to the Grand Canyon Lodge, the main feature of the Grand Canyon Resort complex.

Initially built in the late 1920s, the resort now includes the main lodge and 114 cabins. Overnight guests stay in the cabins, which are detached from the main lodge, which houses a dining room, souvenir store, bar, and other concessions. It is constructed primarily of Ponderosa Pine logs and local Limestone, and is the only complete surviving lodge in the National Parks system. The lodge was added to the National Register of Historic Places in 1982, and designated a National Historic Landmark in 1987.

I typically travel with two cameras: my little Canon pocket camera, and a larger, Nikon Digital SLR camera and two lenses. The pocket camera is great for quick shots and taking pics while I'm riding, the bigger camera is reserved for more scenic shots when stopped. When I got to the Grand Canyon, I took my Nikon out of the saddlebag and put my zoom lens on, hoping to get some good shots of the canyon itself. Ah, but the battery was dead. I always bring an extra battery with me, but, when I swapped the dead battery out, I discovered my extra one was dead, too. Oops. Oh well, I figured I could charge them both overnight once I got to my motel, since I always bring a charger. Well, almost always. Somehow, for this trip, I neglected to pack the charger. So here I was, at the Grand Canyon with a really nice camera and no batteries. The Nikon went back into the saddlebag, and I took pictures with my point-and-shoot Canon, which, by the way, also takes great photos.

Anyway, I played tourist for the next couple of hours, wandering around the area to see the sights and get photos of the Grand Canyon, watching a thunderstorm roll across the North Rim while sitting on the patio outside the Lodge, having an icy cold beer in the Roughrider Saloon, and spending a bit of my cash in the souvenir store.

I still had about seventy-five miles to go to get to my motel, so I decided to head back out to Highway 89A. The temperature had dropped a bit more by this time, so I donned a light jacket and rolled north. Just past the Park Entrance I felt the first raindrops as the thunderstorm began rolling across the landscape. I pulled off and added my raingear, hoping I could beat the heavier rain. By the time I made it to Jacob Lake and the intersection with 89A, the rain was coming heavier, and I figured I would just get wet for the next forty miles or so. Highway 89A heads east out of Jacob Lake and begins a series of sharp twists and turns before making a snaking drop to the desert floor about 3,300 feet below. The Pasture Canyon Lookout point offers a panoramic view of the desert below, and while there is nothing particularly interesting to see, the vast expanse stretching for miles is impressive. By now the rain and hail *(yes, hail!)* had moved on and the sun was pushing its way back through the clouds. Once I hit the desert floor the temperature was climbing rapidly, and by the time I got to my destination for the night I was sweating like crazy!

My home for the next two days was the Cliff Dweller's Lodge, a rustic outpost with lodging, a store, and restaurant. Homesteaders first settled here in the 1920s, and the original structure is still standing at the edge of the property. Sitting at the base of the Vermillion Cliffs, the Lodge is pretty much the only business around for miles. I got checked in, and my room was around the back, with a view of the massive sandstone, limestone, and shale formations. Just outside the door to my room was a small enclosed area that I was thankful for, because as the thunderstorm moved away, a wicked wind came roaring in behind it. I tucked my bike into the small "carport," got unloaded, and checked out the room. Clean, basic, and comfortable, the room had two beds, a table, a bathroom, and a fridge. The TV looked like a 1989 RCA special, but it worked. No wi-fi available out here, so I was unable to check emails, but that was okay too.

The Vermillion Cliffs are part of the Vermillion Cliffs National Monument, which covers just under 300,000 acres. Named for the deep red color of the rock formations in the area, the Monument was created in 2000 by President Clinton from existing land managed by the government. The Monument is now under the care of the US Bureau of Land Management. The actual cliffs run along the eastern and southern edges of the monument, where the cliffs rise as high as 6,500 feet above sea level. Small streams flow through the rocks, providing enough moisture to support wildlife. Some of the wildlife present in the area include hawks, falcons, eagles, and the recently relocated California Condor, an endangered species brought into the area due to the lack of human habitation. Larger animals include bighorn sheep, mountain lions, and pronghorn antelope. In the streams, several rare species of fish have been observed. Human activity dates back thousands of years, with a myriad of Native American pueblos and remains of Native villages spread across the monument. It is even reported that some of the oldest petroglyphs in the United States are located in the Vermillion Cliffs.

I had planned on staying for a couple of days here, mainly to sightsee but also to give myself a chance to rest up in case I needed it. The plan was to take the next day and just putt around the area, seeing what I could see. I had a light dinner that night in the café and went back to my room to check out the maps and see where I would go next. I knew I was in the general vicinity of some of Utah's National Parks, but I honestly was surprised to see that Zion and Bryce Canyon National Parks were actually quite close. Yeah, I know: I admit it, I suck at geography, which is weird with all the traveling that I do. Anyway, I did a little research *(hard to do without internet access and spotty cell service... we are such slaves to technology)*, and discovered that Zion, the closer of the two, is a great park for hiking and walking, while Bryce is more accessible by vehicles. Since walking on uneven terrain or extended hiking was still an issue for me, I decided to make the trip up to Bryce Canyon. The next morning, I saddled up and headed north for the 140-mile jaunt back into Utah. After stopping for breakfast in Kanab, I rolled up US Highway 89 for about sixty miles before turning onto Utah Highway 12. It's just a short run to Utah Highway 63 and a hop to the park entrance. It did take a while to travel that fifteen or so miles due to road construction, but I made it to the Visitor's Center and went inside to refill my water bottle and hit the bathroom.

The Visitor's Center at Bryce Canyon is a really nice, clean, well-laid out building with exhibits, maps, information, and of course the requisite souvenir shop. I grabbed a map and looked at the variety of trails and hikes in the area before I discovered that the park operates a series of shuttle buses that run up the road to various overlook and scenic viewpoints. Included in the entrance fee to the Park, the shuttle buses run every fifteen minutes to the viewpoints. Riders can hop on or off at whichever viewpoint they wish along the eighteen-mile loop through the Park, then catch the next shuttle to the next overlook.

I opted to do that, rather than try to ride to each of the viewpoints myself. The Park has this system down: the bus arrived just outside the Visitor's Center, I hopped on and rode to the first stop. The stops are all well marked on maps inside the bus, as well as the park map I had grabbed earlier. What a way to tour the park! Sure, the bus was crowded sometimes, but if it was too packed, I just waited for the next one.

I'll tell ya, the Grand Canyon was impressive and beautiful, but it's got nothing on Bryce Canyon. The views at the numerous stops were breathtaking! Even though each stop is only a short distance from the previous one, none of the views are the same...or even similar. The colors of the cliffs and valleys are vibrant and bright, there are caves and indentations in the rock faces, and the huge trees at the bottom of the valleys and along the cliffsides only emphasize the grandeur of the scenery. The entire tour will typically take about three hours or more, depending on how long a person wishes to stay at each stop.

Bryce Canyon, UT

I took my time at each of the viewpoints, getting photos and just marveling at God's creation spread out before me. By mid-afternoon, I figured I had better head out. Back at the Visitor's Center, I got out my map and looked at a route back to Marble Canyon. I'm not real big on taking a trip that is just up and back...I love to make a "loop" out of my tours so I can see as much of the area and scenery as possible. I looked for a different way back to the Vermillion Cliffs and decided to split off at Kanab and run east, continuing on US-89 *(instead of US-89A)*. The road runs through the southern part of the Grand Staircase-Escalante National Monument just north of the Utah-Arizona border. Just after crossing into Arizona, I saw a large body of water to my left, which turned out to be Lake Powell.

The lake is a man-made reservoir created by the construction of Glen Canyon Dam in the late 1950s. Situated along the Colorado River, it is the second-largest man-made lake in the United States, surpassed only by Lake Mead in Nevada, also on the Colorado River. The possibility of a dam in Glen Canyon was initially discussed in 1924, but construction of Hoover Dam in 1936 put a stop to the proposed project. Because of growth in the American and Mexican states making up the Colorado River Basin, however, the Bureau of Reclamation resurrected the project and work began on the Glen Canyon Dam in 1956. Construction continued for ten years until its completion in 1966. The Bureau of Reclamation also wanted to construct Echo Park Dam in the Dinosaur National Monument, but environmentalists at the time opposed that project, seeing it as a threat to protected land. The drawn-out battle ended up with the Echo Park project scuttled, and Glen Canyon Dam being built. In 1972, the Glen Canyon National Recreation Area was established, spanning portions of four counties and two states. The area is managed by the National Park Service. The lake serves as water storage and supply for Colorado, Utah, Wyoming, and New Mexico as part of the Colorado River Compact. In the past few years, water levels in Lake Powell and Lake Mead have dropped to dangerously low stages, often only about half of what they normally would be. This lack of water was clearly evident as I stopped and looked at the lake. Recent studies have deemed that water levels in the two lakes will never reach original levels.

I stopped for gas in Page, about six miles further, and decided to eat there, rather than at the café at my motel. There were a couple of reasons for this, but primarily because last night's dinner had been a patty melt, dinner salad, and a beer...and cost me over twenty bucks. The other reason was, I was hungry! Seeing nothing but fast-food joints around, I asked the gas station attendant if there was anywhere to get "real" food...he told me about a place just around the corner behind a couple of big-name hotels, with "family dining."

I found the Gone West Family Restaurant in a small strip mall behind the Burger King and next to a Holiday Inn Express. Clean, wide-open, and spacious, the restaurant was not very full, and I was immediately greeted by a hostess who directed me to a table. A side note: Being greeted and welcomed by restaurant staff is always a good sign to me, as I cannot count how many times servers and hostesses have looked at the road-weary, dirty biker in front of them and promptly seated me as far away from the front of the restaurant *(and other patrons)* as possible.

A tall glass of frosty iced tea appeared on my table and I ordered a pork chop dinner for a very reasonable fourteen dollars. The waiter directed me to the help-yourself all-you-can-eat salad bar and rushed off the get my order to the kitchen. About ten minutes later, a plate with potatoes, gravy, corn on the cob, a dinner roll, and a huge pork chop was delivered to my table. Seriously, this chop was damn near half a pig...and even better, was cooked perfectly! The service was top-notch as well, my glass never got empty, and the waiter made sure to check on me a couple of times to make sure I was happy with my meal.

With my belly stuffed and my gas tank full, I headed south on US-89 down to the valley floor at Hidden Springs and turned west onto US-89A for the run back to Marble Canyon. I made a detour at Lee's Ferry to go down to the Colorado River since it was still pushing triple digits and I was getting warm. I parked the scoot and walked down to the river's edge, took off my boots and waded into the rushing waters. Holy crap, that water was cold! I waded up to my knees and stood there looking downriver through the canyon, amazed at the contradiction of this raging, freezing river cutting through the middle of the parched and hot desert. By the time I rode back to the motel, thirteen miles away, my jeans were completely dry, and I was beat. My plans for a day of short rides around the area having been dashed, I grabbed a cold beer at the small store at the resort and called it a day.

CHAPTER SIXTEEN

While I was looking at the maps, I was listening to the radio and an Eagles song came on. In one of my "oooh, shiny red ball" moments, I looked to see how far I was from Winslow, Arizona. Winslow is featured in a song called "Take It Easy," the Eagles' first radio hit from 1972. One of the lyric lines is "I'm standin' on the corner in Winslow Arizona, it's such a fine sight to see. There's a girl, my Lord, in a flatbed Ford slowin' down to take a look at me." Little did songwriters Glenn Frey and Jackson Browne realize what that song would do for the town of Winslow. Due to the popularity of the song Winslow is now home to the Standin' on the Corner Park. The park *(basically a city street corner)* is comprised of a mural, a life-sized bronze statue of a man holding a guitar, and a flatbed Ford truck parked along the curb. The park is surrounded by a brick wall with each of the donor's names on them. Built by a consortium known as the Standin' on the Corner Foundation, the park was built not only to honor the mention of the town in song, but to spark a renaissance of the city itself, having been bypassed by the completion of Interstate 40 in 1977. The Foundation formed in 1997 and got to work planning the park and rounding up donations. The park was opened in September of 1999.

From where I was staying, Winslow was a mere 175 miles or so away. Easy enough, but my plan was to ride east and north through the arid, desolate Arizona desert, hit the Four Corners National Monument, then stay in Cortez, Colorado. The 175 miles would have been no big deal, but that was 175 miles each way, then more mileage to get up to Cortez. By the time I looked at tweaking the itinerary, it would have made for a 450-mile plus day, and after doing about 300 miles the day before, my broken body just would not take that kind of abuse…I mean, mileage. Not only that, but in between Winslow and Cortez, there was virtually no place to spend the night that I could find.

It sucks to have to admit my limitations to myself, but I have learned, since the crash, what my limits are and not to push it too far. Prior to the crash, I would have done it without a second thought. The reality is, if I had decided to make the side trip to Winslow, I would likely have been laid up for two or three days in Cortez. Winslow would have to wait.

With temperatures forecast to be in the low 100s, I headed off from Marble Canyon and sailed through the cool desert morning back up to Page, where I gassed up and grabbed a quick bite of breakfast. Just east of Page on Arizona Highway 98, I passed a huge industrial plant of some kind off to my left. I later came to find out that this was the Salt River Project- Navajo Generating Station, a 2.25-gigawatt coal-fired power plant. Situated on Navajo Nation land, it was responsible for providing power to Arizona, Nevada, and California, as well as pumping Colorado River water to central and southern Arizona. Construction on the site began in 1970, with generating plants being completed between 1974 and 1976. Leases to operate the facility were to run until 2019, with extensions possible until 2044. Operators of the plant, however, decided to close at the end of the lease in 2019. The Navajo Nation began efforts to buy the factory to keep it in operation, but they abandoned the idea in March of 2019. The plant ceased operation in November of 2019, and decommissioning began, with an estimated three years to completion.

Highway 98 was interesting…not so much for the scenery, but because at each of the few rest areas/turnouts along the route, there were Native American vendors selling their wares: necklaces, jewelry, knives, leather goods, and so on. Typically, the vendors were set up with a table under a tent-type cover, with their creations spread out.

I stopped at a few of them along my travels through Arizona, and the one I pulled into along Highway 89 had some beautiful stuff. I have always been a fan of turquoise and ended up buying myself a ring made of turquoise and sterling silver. The lady selling things was also busy making more jewelry as she passed the time and said that her products were all made by herself or family members. One item that caught my eye, but was unfortunately out of my price range, was a gorgeous bone-handled knife with a hand-tooled leather sheath. If it had not been $200, I would have bought it! It was well worth every penny.

US-89 near Page, AZ

Highway 89 came to an end at the junction with US-160, and the road took me northeast up to a small stop called Mexican Water. The only thing of note, hell, the only thing period, in Mexican Water that I could see was the trading post, which is a Sinclair gas station, cafe and quickie mart. I topped off my fuel, refilled my water bottle, and pulled back onto the highway. There really is not much civilization out here, more like small outposts where a school, gas station, medical clinic, and things like that are located. I rolled into what was likely the largest of these outposts, a place called Teec Nos Pos. Navajo for "Cottonwoods in a circle," Teec Nos Pos covers about fourteen square miles with an estimated 730 people. It is known as a "census designated place," which is described by the United States Census Bureau as a concentration of population for statistical purposes only. The racial makeup of Teec Nos Pos is reported to be 96.5% Native and 1% white.

About six miles further up the road was the Arizona-New Mexico State Line, but more importantly for my interests, was the Four Corners National Monument.

The Four Corners is where the borders of Arizona, New Mexico, Colorado, and Utah all come together, and is the only place in the United States where four states merge at one point. Maintained as a tourist attraction by the Navajo Nation, the site is basically a large gravel lot. Admission is five dollars. There really is not much here, other than the marker designating the exact spot where the four states join borders. There is a small visitor's center, the "carousel," which is a courtyard of sorts surrounding the marker with several booths where people sell their crafts. A sandstone marker was originally placed in 1875, but by 1899 that marker was broken. It was replaced by surveyors, and in 1912 a concrete pad was poured around it. By 1931, the new marker was also damaged and deteriorated, so a brass disk was installed. The Bureau of Land Management and the Bureau of Indian Affairs installed a raised concrete pad around the brass marker, with the names and boundaries of the states carved in tile. The site was rebuilt in 1992, and the brass disk was replaced with a plate of bronze and aluminum and set into granite. Each state's seal is noted in the respective boundaries, and each state's flag flies over it. One additional rebuild of the site took place in 2010, but the disk installed in 1992 remains. This area has been home to native peoples for thousands of years, and archaeologists have recorded numerous ancient Puebloan sites dating prior to AD 1300 throughout the Four Corners area

I parked the bike in the gravel and walked up to the monument, standing in line with about fifty other people to get a look at, and pictures of, the marker. Thankfully, the line moved fairly quickly, as there was no shade, and it was pushing 102 degrees. A lady in front of me graciously offered to take my picture at the monument after she was done doing the same with her kids. I wandered through the vendors, looking at more Native jewelry, t-shirts, souvenirs, and other wares for sale. Back in the parking lot, I noticed two old, small vacation-style trailers selling Indian Tacos and fry bread. I could not pass up the fry bread…. fresh, hot, and chewy…even in the 100+ degree heat!

I had been told by people that the Four Corners is not much to see, other than the coolness factor of four states bordering each other in one spot. They were right, it really is nothing more than a gravel lot surrounded by 25,000 acres of Navajo land. But it was really cool to see, and well worth stopping in. I got back on the road and sliced through the northwesternmost corner of New Mexico for less than a mile before crossing into Colorado and the final run into the city of Cortez, my destination for the night. Glad to be off the road and out of the heat, I checked into my motel, grabbed a cold beverage, and unloaded the bike. I found a terrific Mexican restaurant just down the road for chips, salsa, and a taco salad…oh, and a beer or two. Perfect end to a tremendous, but ridiculously hot, day.

Standing in four states at once

CHAPTER SEVENTEEN

I rolled out of Cortez the next morning with a full gas tank, heading east toward Durango on US-160. I didn't head out real early, as my plan for the day was only about 250 miles or so, but I was early enough on this Sunday morning that traffic was at a minimum. The sun was out, and the temperature was nice and mild. I made my way through Durango without any issues and turned onto US-550 northbound into the Rockies. US Highway 550 stretches from New Mexico into Colorado, and the Colorado portion runs along the high western edge of the Continental Divide.

There is a section of this highway that runs between the towns of Silverton and Ouray called the "Million Dollar Highway." A short twenty-five miles in length, the road is part of the San Juan Scenic Byway and is rated by many media outlets as one of the twelve most dangerous roads in the world, in company with Bolivia's Death Road and the Highway of Death in Iraq. If that weren't enough, it also boasts the highest avalanche hazard per mile in North America. Riding out of Durango, the climb began as I headed north toward Silverton, a former silver mining camp founded in 1874. Now the County Seat, it is the only incorporated community in San Juan County, and home to about 700 people. It also claims to be one of the highest towns in the US, sitting at over 9,300 feet above sea level. The road became increasingly curvier as I climbed out of Durango *(6,500 feet)*, especially the last twenty miles or so as I dropped *(yes... descended, dropped, lowered)* into Silverton. Stopping at a quickie mart/gas station for a quick break, I thought, "well, hell, that wasn't so bad. What's the big deal about the Million Dollar Highway?" I got out my map to see where I was going to go as I left, and that's when I realized: I had not ridden the Million Dollar Highway yet! Double checking my map with one hanging in the gas station window, I confirmed that I was just at the start of it, not the end.

The road started out easy enough, until the first sharp turns a few miles up. Tight turns, switchbacks, and hairpins dominated the next twenty-two miles with steep, rocky cliffs on my left and sheer drop-offs to God-knows-where on my right. To add to the fun, guardrails are non-existent. The Colorado Department of Transportation says there is no room for guardrails due to snow removal in the winter months…plows simply push the snow off the mountain.

According to one author, the highway's stretch south of Ouray is "steep, twisting and completely unforgiving of driver error." He is right. The road is a twisting, serpentine thread of two- lane asphalt that climbs and dips through the San Juan Mountains, containing three mountain passes: Red Mountain Pass at 11,018 feet, Molas Pass at 10,970 feet, and Coal Bank Pass at a mere 10,640 feet. The drop-offs are dizzying. The turns are sharp, the lanes are narrow, and the posted speed limits range from 15 mph to a fast-paced 35 mph, but most of the time it is posted at 25 mph. In what will probably be the understatement of this book, the views are incredibly stunning. Unfortunately, I did not get to see a lot of it as I was focused on not sending myself and my bike into the abyss below. There are a few turnouts along the way, and I availed myself of them to get pictures of the grandeur displayed before me. Sadly, the pictures I did manage to take are no match for the views in person. The jagged peaks of the mountains, the meandering ribbon of asphalt, and the absolute drop-offs plunging into the canyons simply cannot be captured in a photograph. The next time I ride this road, I will have a video camera attached to the bike! On the road, I had to watch for not only the upcoming curves, but rocks, animals, and other vehicles. This area is home to a myriad of wildlife: black bear, deer, mountain goats, elk and more, and they are known to make their way onto the roadway at times. The weather can always be a concern in this part of the state, as it can change in a moment's notice without warning. Fortunately, I experienced sunny, warm, clear weather all the way through, with temperatures on the passes hovering in the mid-sixties and pushing into the eighties by the time I hit Ouray.

Even as an experienced rider, this road required all of my attention. Not just because of the aforementioned hazards, but also because US-550 is one of only two north-south US Highways in the state. Yes, I also had to watch for other cars, semi-trucks, buses, and the ever-ominous mega-motorhome commandos navigating the narrow road as well. The good news is, the road is very well maintained, the pavement is mostly smooth and clear of debris and gravel on the turns. Colorado is aware that this is a popular road, especially for motorcycles, and they do their best to keep it safe. Not only that, but in the twenty-two-mile stretch, I saw more State Police and County Sheriff's vehicles than I did on the entire rest of my ride through Colorado. They don't mess around up here…you speed, you get ticketed. The nice part of it was, even though my attention was focused on the road itself, the low speed made for a relaxing but adrenaline-filled run.

I will make a confession right here: There is not much in this world that scares me. Two things do. The first one, inexplicably, is the Marquam Bridge in Portland, Oregon. Part of Interstate 5, the double-decker bridge spans 400 feet across the Willamette River, roughly 130 feet below. It is often considered Oregon's busiest bridge, with well over 150,000 vehicles crossing it daily. I don't know why, but every time I have crossed that bridge *(either in a cage or on a bike)* I have been terrified. It does not matter whether I am on the top deck or lower deck, crossing that bridge for me is thirty seconds of sheer, white-knuckled terror. To a much lesser degree, the second thing that gives me the willies is a curving mountain road with no safety barriers and drop-offs into the pits of Hell. I rode this stretch of highway close to the yellow line and because of the acute turns, barely got out of second gear. The fastest I ever got in my twenty-five-mile ride through this part of the Rockies was 40 mph, and only for about three seconds on a rare straightaway. I know there are some sport bike riders out there who will want to carve the turns and shred the passes as fast as they can. Good for them, but statistics tell another story: in the ten years between 2005 and 2015, there were 412 accidents and eight fatalities…and most involved single vehicle crashes. Failing to negotiate one of the many turns on a bike will almost certainly result in a fatality. And remember, the police love this stretch of road for boosting their revenue.

The name of the road is a matter of contention and folklore. One story is that the road, when constructed in the 1880s, cost one million dollars per mile to build. Another says that the fill dirt used contains a million dollars in gold ore. Still another relates the story of an early traveler who was so overwhelmed by vertigo while traveling the highway that he would never do it again, not even for a million dollars.

I dropped down into the town of Ouray *(about 7,800 feet)* and felt it was time to enjoy a celebratory ice-cold beverage…not to mention a little break to ease my adrenaline levels. Ouray is often called the Switzerland of America as it is encircled by the San Juan Mountains, with peaks reaching 13,000 feet elevation. So far, my day had been spent at elevations above 10,000 feet and less than 40 mph. I think I had ridden more mountain passes and taken more turns on this day than I had in the past couple of years combined! Being that it was a warm, sunny summer day, the town and all its bars and restaurants were packed, but I was able to find a spot at a small eatery where I could enjoy my beer.

My plan was to continue on to Glenwood Springs and spend the night, but when I was researching motel rooms there, I discovered the innkeepers must have been very proud of their rooms. It was almost impossible to find a room for less than $100, and I'm too damn cheap to pay that much for a bed and a shower. I stopped in Montrose for gas and jumped onto US-50 for a while, then took a slight spur on Colorado 141 up to Interstate 70. About 135 miles later I came to Parachute, a town of about 1,100 people on Parachute Creek, near the Colorado River. I saw a couple of motels and decided to stop and check them out. Neither one was the typical type of place I like: motor court style motels where I can park right in front of my room, but they were worth a look. The first one didn't impress me at all, with a couple of broken-down cars in the parking lot and the like, but the second one looked promising…and sounded expensive.

The Grand Vista Hotel was a medium-sized facility that offered large rooms, indoor pool, hot tub, and a bar. When I checked with the desk clerk for availability, she said they had a king room available, for $75 a night. Deal! She was nice enough to allow me to park the bike directly out front, under the canopy *(and the cameras)*. I got the bike unpacked, figuring I could get settled in my room and hit the bar for a drink. Sadly, the bar was closed on Sundays and Mondays. Oh, well. But the good news was that they had a guest laundry, so I threw all my dirty, road worn clothes in the laundry while I went for a swim *(a quick note: swimming is one of the few "real" exercises I can do that do not put undue strain on my injuries while still burning calories and getting my heart rate up)*. A quick walk to the store about a block away and my refreshment needs were met. Like a lot of little towns, food offerings were typical: fast food, gas stations, and a couple of mom-and-pop restaurants. Again, it was Sunday, so a few of the little places were closed, except for the tiny Mexican restaurant a block or so away, and a place called Shommy's across the freeway. I opted for the latter, having just had Mexican food the previous night. It took a bit to find Shommy's, as it is tucked into a gas station/mini-mart, but find it I did and went in. It is a small place, maybe fifteen tables or so and a little ten-seat bar. Typical traveler fare: burgers, sandwiches, salads, but also comfort food staples: meat loaf, pork chops, fried chicken *(yum!)* and the like. The server, Jenn, was cute as can be and friendly, and I asked her what her honest opinion of their fried chicken was. She said, "couldn't tell ya…never had it." She then went on to say that everyone loves it, it's one of their most popular dishes; and the cook that was on duty was the best cook they have. Okay then, fried chicken it was! Expectations were low, but I was more than pleasantly surprised. The chicken was some of the best I have ever had. Crispy, hot, juicy, and cooked perfectly. I had wanted the mashed potatoes and gravy with it, but they were out of mashed potatoes *(???)*, so I got a baked potato with all the fixin's and "steamed vegetables": broccoli, cauliflower, carrots. Yeah, I didn't eat those, but the tater was good! Fifteen bucks later I toddled my fat, happy ass across to the quickie mart to grab a beer for later and made my way back to the hotel to settle in for the night.

Thunderstorms skirted the area all night, so I was happy to see the clear, blue sky the next morning as I loaded up my scoot for the day. Before I could hit the road, however, I had a little business to attend to. Since my Nikon camera was out of commission due to dead batteries and no charger, and I had decided to lighten the load, I filled a small package with the camera, zoom lens, batteries, and a couple of souvenirs. Just up the street from the hotel was the Post Office, and I got there just as they opened. Fifteen minutes later, my package was on its way back home, and I was ready to hit the road. Again, mild temperatures started the day and I headed west on Interstate 70 for a few miles until I got to Rifle *(honest, that's the town's name)* and exited the superslab in favor of Colorado Highway 13 which took me north through the remainder of Colorado. It was a pretty uneventful ride…maybe I should say, it was a pretty, uneventful ride, because it was both: Pretty and uneventful.

Well, almost. I hit a few spots of road construction, one to the point where the highway was nothing more than a dirt track reduced to one lane with a pilot car leading the way. I was one of the very few vehicles on the road, and I noticed the flagger say something into his radio as I approached. By now the temperature had climbed into the mid-eighties or so, and not only was it hot, it was dusty from the road crew. I stopped and shut off the bike while waiting for the pilot car, but when it came back it waited a minute before leading me and the beat-up old Dodge pickup in front of me. It turns out that the flagger called for a water truck to go ahead of us and knock the dust down so I wouldn't inhale 632 pounds of Colorado's finest dirt. We began to move, and as I passed the flagger, he gave me the "biker's wave," two fingers pointed down. I returned the gesture and gave silent thanks for fellow riders. The dirt track stretched about a mile or so, and then it was on to brand new, freshly laid asphalt.

At the state line entering Wyoming, the highway designation changed to Wyoming Highway 789 and I encountered the town of Baggs. Truth be told, calling Baggs a "town" is a stretch...it covers less than one square mile, and is reportedly home to 400 people... more of a village. But they do have a Conoco gas station there, so I decided to stop and top off the tank and refill my water bottle. You have heard of places that "if you blink, you'll miss it" ... I think the idea came from Baggs. Highway 789 runs the entire north-south length of Wyoming, from Colorado to Montana. After leaving Baggs, there is a whole lot of nothing for the next fifty miles, where the two-lane track intersects Interstate 80. It is desolate, barren country, with mostly open range land for grazing cattle. The only sign of civilization I saw after leaving Baggs was another road crew working on the highway, this stretch was not as bad as the last one I encountered, but it was still three miles of grated, grooved asphalt. I hit I-80 and made the short twenty-four-mile run into Rawlins.

I found a small, mom-and-pop motel in West Rawlins, called Motel 7 *(so clever)*. It was old, but clean, and the price was right. Run by a Pakistani/East Indian couple, they had updated the best they could. The room was small but comfortable; the air conditioner, stuffed into what had once been a large window, cranked out ice cold air, and the bathroom was clean. I was not sure I would fit into the tiny shower, but the water pressure was good. I unpacked the bike and decided to go hunting for a place to have dinner later, and a beer now.

Rawlins, the County Seat of Carbon County, is a city of about 10,000 people that has definitely seen better days. Incorporated in 1886, Rawlins is named after Union General John Rawlins who was camping in the area in 1867. He told his men he wanted some "cold, clear water" to drink. His scouts searched the vicinity and found a spring in the hills that surround the location of the city. According to local folklore, he professed it was the most refreshing drink he had ever tasted and that if anything were ever to be named after him, he wanted it to be a spring of water. The commander of the survey party immediately designated it Rawlins Springs. The community that began to grow nearby retained the name, until 1866 when it was incorporated, and the name shortened to Rawlins. Copper mining was instrumental in the town's growth, and in 1901 a newly built state prison opened in Rawlins, built from locally quarried sandstone. Relocated to a new facility just south of the city in 1980, the Wyoming State Prison is now the largest employer in Rawlins.

In the 1920s, the Producers and Refiners Corporation built a refinery and company outpost five miles east of Rawlins, and named the new community Parco. The town and refinery were bought out by Sinclair Oil Company in 1934 and renamed Sinclair. The 1950s and 1960s saw the discovery and mining of uranium ore, and the 1990s were coal-mining years for the county. The uranium mines have mostly been decommissioned. The coal mines produced over four million tons of coal from the various open surface and underground mines. The boom-and-bust years have been hard on Rawlins, and it shows. Today, natural gas and coal production still continues in the county.

Like most any city, there is a big difference between "old" Rawlins and "new" Rawlins. The western part appears to be the "old," and several dilapidated motels, restaurants and other businesses stand testament to a once-booming town. "New" Rawlins is on the eastern side, where numerous highways merge. Interstate 80; US-30; US-287; Wyoming Highways 789, 71, and 76 all merge or run concurrently on the east end of the city. Here is where the newer chain hotels, chain restaurants, fast food, and Walmart are located.

I decided to do some exploring, looking for somewhere to get dinner and maybe a local bar for a cold beer. I found a sports bar/restaurant downtown called Buck's that was busy, even at three in the afternoon. I parked the bike and made my way to the back of the room, where the bar was located. I took the only remaining stool that was available, and in no time had a frosty mug of beer in front of me. I spent the next hour or so with my beer and generously over-salted peanuts, visiting with a long-distance trucker from Alabama sitting next to me, telling tales and lies of our adventures on the road. He lamented he didn't really get time to ride his bike, an old FXR that he had bought new. He said he spent so much time crisscrossing the country in his truck that he rarely got time to ride when he was home.

I got back to my motel and caught up on some emails and other business. I also did a little maintenance check on the bike: making sure the oil was up, the lights all worked, the belt was intact, and so on. I discovered that my high beam bulb in my headlight had fallen out. I have aftermarket LED bulbs in my headlamp, and the high beam wanted to keep falling out of its perch. After messing with it for an hour or so, I took it out and stuck it in my saddlebag; then headed out for dinner. I had seen a few places that would have worked: a repurposed Denny's-type building called Cappy's; a stand-alone restaurant called the Big City Grille *(the "e" on the end makes it fancier, you know)*; and a Chinese place known as the Four Seasons. I rolled up to the Big City Grille at about 5:30pm, and the place was locked up tight. Strike one. Next was Cappy's, looking like a place for home-cookin' type dinners, but they too, were closed. At least this one had a sign on the door: "Closed Mondays & Tuesdays." Damn, strike two. Unfortunately, the same thing happened with the Four Seasons. Evidently, people in Rawlins don't eat out much on Mondays and Tuesdays.

By now, I was starving! I headed back downtown to the one place I knew would be open: Buck's Sports Grill. The place was packed! I was able to find a seat at the bar once again and ordered a bacon cheeseburger and fries...and another beer. The burger was surprisingly good, the fries were even better, and the best thing yet was that their 16-ounce Pabst Blue Ribbon cans were a buck apiece. Yeah, I know, it's PBR, but what the hell---I'll drink 'em all day long if they're a buck. My tab for dinner, two beers and a tip came to a whopping fifteen dollars.

Back at the motel, I got my shop towel out of the saddlebag and scrubbed the remains of the dead bugs and insects off my windshield and lights. Certifying my scoot was ready to roll, I headed inside just as the thunderstorm rolled through. Within five minutes, the clear sky had turned black, the wind came up, and the rumbles of thunder and peals of lightning streaked across the sky. The first room-shaking "BOOM" knocked the power out, so I stood in my doorway watching the storm pass by until the power came on about ten minutes later. Good thing I had a flashlight in my tool kit...

CHAPTER EIGHTEEN

It was time to say goodbye to Rawlins, and I got loaded up, gassed up, and saddled up to hit the road. Heading north on US-287, I thought I might be able to stop at the Wyoming Frontier Prison, but they weren't open yet, and I was itching to get some wind in my face. Not too far out of town, I saw a lone road sign off to the right. As I pulled up, it said "Continental Divide, 7,004 feet," so of course I stopped to get a picture. It was not the last time I would encounter such a sign, as I seemed to be crossing the Divide back and forth all along my travels through Colorado, Wyoming and Montana. I don't really know if I would call this terrain "desert," but I do know it was barren, dry, and empty. After about forty-five miles I turned onto Wyoming Highway 220 and continued my ride north.

In the middle of nowhere, up sprang Independence Rock State Historic Site. Surprisingly, since I had seen no other vehicles of any kind in the past hour, there were several cars and RVs in the parking lot. Since I was in no hurry, and had no time frame to adhere to, I stopped in to check it out.

A short distance away from the parking lot, I saw what looked like a large mound rising from the ground. Early descriptions said it looked like a "large elephant up to its sides in mud"; "a big bowl turned upside down"; and "an irregular loaf of bread raised very light

& cracked & creased in all ways." Even more descriptions likened it to a turtle, an apple cut in half and laid upside down, and more.

Near Rawlins, WY

Used as a landmark of sorts by the various Indian Tribes of the Central Rockies; including the Shoshone, Crow, Pawnee, Arapaho, Cheyenne, Blackfeet, and others; the giant rock came to be known as the Painted Rock due to their carvings. Independence Rock is made of granite, and is approximately 130 feet tall, 1,900 feet long, and 850 feet wide. From the 1820s to the 1850s, fur traders and mountain men used the huge rock rising up from the Sweetwater Valley floor as a landmark as well. How the site got its current name is disputed, but the best evidence shows that pioneer William Sublette christened the rock in 1830 as he and his caravan of eighty-one men and ten wagons passed by on their way to Wind River. In the middle of the 1800s, it was once again used as a prominent landmark for the Mormon, California, and Oregon Emigrant Trails, as well as the Pony Express Road. Pioneers felt that the monolith designated the Eastern border of the Rocky Mountains, and felt that if they could arrive there by the Fourth of July, they could make it to their Western destinations before winter set in. Although many of the early inscriptions and carvings into the stone have been worn away by time, wind, and dust storms, many of the deeper engraved names and images are preserved. Wyoming's first Masonic Lodge meeting was held on the site on July 4, 1862. Designated as a State Historical Site in 1961, the park is now managed by the State of Wyoming.

Independence Rock, WY

Back on the road I skirted the edge of the Pathfinder National Wildlife Refuge, a 16,000-plus acre site managed jointly by the US Fish and Wildlife Service and the US Bureau of Reclamation. The area includes the Pathfinder Reservoir and is home to Pronghorn antelope and a variety of migratory birds.

I rolled into Casper just about noon, and needed to gas up, refill my water bottle, and grab a bite. Casper is not a huge city, it has a population of about 57,000, so it was fairly easy to navigate. I grabbed a cheeseburger at a fast-food joint for a buck, then went looking for the Harley dealer. Oil City Harley-Davidson is a small store, with friendly employees and a well-laid out showroom. I was there just long enough to grab a few souvenirs and take a peek at my map before the next leg of my trip up to Buffalo.

Unfortunately, the trip from Casper to Buffalo was 112 miles of freeway on Interstate 25. I looked for side roads and back roads to avoid some or all of the superslab, but no such luck. Granted, the posted speed limit in that part of Wyoming is 80 mph, so I was only looking at about ninety minutes or so, but still…when you dislike freeways as much as I do, I was not looking forward to the ride. I set out and hit the multi-lane pavement, set the cruise control, and blasted my way north. The terrain was not much to look at and traffic was less than minimal, so it was kind of a mind-numbing ride…for about seventy miles. I saw a sign for the little burg of Kaycee, along with one that said, "Gotta see this! Chris LeDoux Park." What the hell, I needed to break up the boredom somehow.

For those of you who don't know Chris LeDoux, he was a country music and rodeo star, whose son, Ned, is also a country music singer. Born in 1948 in Biloxi, MS, Chris would often visit his grandparents' farm near Kaycee where he learned to ride horses. At age thirteen he entered his first rodeo and was soon winning junior competitions. He moved to Cheyenne and won the Wyoming State Rodeo Championship bareback riding title twice while in high school, earning a scholarship to Casper College. In 1970, Chris became a professional rodeo rider, and to help pay his expenses sold homemade tapes of his music out of the back of his pickup truck. He won the world Bareback Riding Championship in 1976 at the National Finals Rodeo in Oklahoma.

Upon his retirement from the rodeo in 1980, LeDoux and his family moved to Kaycee and he began focusing on his music career, playing concerts and recording albums on his own label. He released twenty-two albums on his own during the 1980s. Things changed in 1989, when he was mentioned in a Garth Brooks song *(Much Too Young [To Feel This Damn Old])* and Chris signed with a subsidiary of Capitol Records. Over the next eleven years, he released six more albums, and won a Grammy for Best Country Vocal Collaboration for his duet with Garth Brooks from his debut album. LeDoux was diagnosed with a form of cancer in 2000 and underwent a liver transplant, then went on to record two more albums. His cancer returned and eventually cost him his life in 2005 at age fifty-six. He was posthumously inducted into the Pro Rodeo Hall of Fame in 2005 and was the first person to be inducted in multiple categories: one for his bareback riding and one "notable" category for his musical contributions.

The hamlet of Kaycee, while small *(population 275),* has a colorful history of its own. Formed in 1906, the new settlement was named after the KC Ranch, but the government required the name of a town to be spelled out, rather than just initials. A post office and a general store were the first businesses to open. Despite warnings of encroaching on Lakota and Arapaho hunting grounds nearby, pioneer Jim Bozeman created the Bozeman Trail, which connected the valuable gold rush territory to the Oregon Trail.

In the late 1800s, during the Indian Wars, two military outposts, Fort Reno and Cantonment Reno were established near the Powder River. Nearby, in the foothills of the Big Horn Mountains, Hole in the Wall became a hideout for the likes of Butch Cassidy's Wild Bunch Gang, Kid Curry, Black Jack Ketchum, and more. They often met at a log cabin to hide and stay out of sight for a while when needed. *(The cabin, built in 1883, is now preserved at the Old Trail Town Museum in Cody, WY.)* The location was perfect for them as no one was able to approach the cabin without alerting those inside. At its peak, Hole in the Wall was comprised of numerous cabins, a corral, livestock, and a livery stable, all maintained by the outlaws.

Perhaps the most infamous part of Kaycee's history is the Johnson County Cattle War. As most of the land was part of the public domain, homesteaders and cattle ranchers set up shop. In the spring, the cows and calves from each ranch were separated and brought in for a roundup. Sometimes, calves would get separated, taken by other ranchers and branded as their own. The large ranches subsequently banned their employees from owning their own cattle. After a particularly brutal winter in 1886, the larger company ranches began to control the flow of water in the area, as well as aggressively seizing public land, and justifying their actions in the name of preventing cattle rustling. They also tried to exclude the smaller ranches from the roundup, as well as killing alleged rustlers.

Organized as the Wyoming Stock Growers Association, the large ranchers hired fifty mercenaries from Texas in 1892 as an attempt to replace the government in Johnson County. To avoid anyone sending an alarm, the telegraph wires were cut.

Nate Champion of the KC Ranch was the mercenaries' first target, because Champion was working with the smaller ranchers to organize a competing roundup. Two other men staying at Champion's cabin were captured when they came out to collect water from the Powder River, and a third man was shot in the doorway of the cabin. The remaining occupant, Champion, refused to give up. Two riders who were passing by saw what was happening and set out to get the Sheriff from Buffalo, about fifty miles away. In the subsequent battle, Champion killed four of the mercenaries and wounded many others. Surprisingly, he kept a journal of what was happening during the siege. Outnumbered and outgunned, Champion attempted to escape out the back door with his journal in his pocket once the invaders had set fire to his house. He exited the house with a rifle in one hand and a revolver in the other but was gunned down by four men who put 28 bullets into his chest. They then pinned a note on Champion's body that read "Cattle Thieves Beware." They also removed pages from the journal that contained the names of some of the vigilantes. The battle came to an end when Johnson County Sheriff William Angus arrived with 200 posse members and confronted the hired killers.

Today, Kaycee is a sedate little place, with Chris LeDoux park commanding attention at the center of town. A larger-than-life sculpture of LeDoux astride his horse, Stormy Weather, lies at the center of the small park. The sculpture was created over two years by Michael Thomas and weighs over 3,500 pounds. The base of the sculpture is a representation of Chris' guitar. When the park and statue were unveiled in 2010, Kaycee was inundated with over 4,000 people.

Chris LeDoux Park; Kaycee, WY

CHAPTER NINETEEN

After spending some time in Kaycee, I headed back onto the superslab for the final run to Buffalo, forty-five miles away. Buffalo is an awesome city of about 4,600 people and lies at the confluence of I-25 and I-90, as well as US-16. Not your typical struggling, decaying small town, Buffalo is thriving, clean and friendly. In addition to two major freeways nearby, there would appear to be a few reasons for Buffalo's success: energy production, including methane production in the nearby Powder River Basin; agriculture; and tourism. Buffalo's location at the foot of the Bighorn Mountains makes it a perfect jumping off point for hikers, campers, hunters, and fishermen. Cattle and sheep ranches flourish in the area as well, due to the fertile nature of the land, and many of the ranches are generational, family-owned spreads. The small city has become one of my favorite small municipalities ever.

I love small towns, and have been through countless ones in my travels. Most of them are typically in various states of decline, with empty storefronts, dilapidated and crumbling buildings, deteriorating infrastructure and so on. Not in Buffalo. As I entered on Main Street *(no kidding)*, I rode directly through the downtown core of the city. I saw maybe two empty storefronts. People were walking the sidewalks, the street and sidewalks were clean, and the small city park was inviting, manicured and maintained. Buffalo was one of the few places where I had made reservations for lodging, as it was to be my home for the next five days. I went looking for my motel and found it a few blocks off Main Street on Highway 16. The Mountain View Motel and RV Park is an older business, and really does not look like much from the outside. Built in the 1920s, the motel is a combination of small log cabins, tent camp sites and RV sites with full hookups. A good-sized courtyard in the center of things offers two gas grills, seating and a firepit. The cabin I had rented was just the right size, with a seriously comfortable bed, TV, mini-fridge, microwave, and bathroom. Fortunately, they also had a coin-op guest laundry available. I checked in with Melissa, who was probably the friendliest innkeeper I have ever encountered and got settled into my room.

The reason for my extended stay in Buffalo was two-fold: one, I wanted to ride around the area and do some exploring; but also, because over the next week, Buffalo was going to be a city with two identities, the other being the town of Durant, Wyoming.

Durant, Wyoming is the fictional home of Absaroka Cunty Sheriff Walt Longmire, a character created by author Craig Johnson, who lives just outside of Buffalo in tiny Ucross *(population 25)*. Johnson based his Longmire series of books and subsequent TV show in a town modeled after Buffalo and named it Durant. Longmire is a lawman of the West who does not like technology, prefers to do things the old-school ways, but must also play politics at times to keep his job. The book series, now eighteen books long, is immensely popular and has garnered Johnson numerous awards and commendations.

In 2012, the A&E Network premiered a series based on the books, and with Johnson's input to keep things in sync, the series took off. It quickly became the highest rated scripted series in the network's history. After the show's third season, A&E suddenly announced the cancellation of the show. Rumors began flying that the network, despite the high ratings, wanted to make more room for "reality" programming. What really happened, however, was that A&E wanted to buy ownership of the show, thereby controlling cost and production, but Warner Horizon Television, knowing the gold mine they had on their hands, refused to sell. A&E retaliated by abruptly cancelling the series outright.

Warner Horizon immediately got to work offering the show to other networks, and it was picked up by Netflix, where it ran for another three seasons. Airing the show on Netflix only increased its popularity, as it was now available to a vastly greater number of people. Actors for the series include Australian-born actor Robert

Taylor as Longmire, Lou Diamond Phillips, A Martinez, Katee Sackhoff, Zahn McClarnon, Cassidy Freeman, and many more.

Since Buffalo was the model for Durant, in 2012 a local gallery owner pitched the idea to use the Longmire character to boost tourism downtown. Longmire Days was born and has been growing ever since. It is estimated that over 10,000 people now visit Buffalo/Durant for Longmire Days, with the attendance increasing every year.

As the event has grown, so have the expectations, yet the Chamber of Commerce and Mr. Johnson have done a great job of keeping up. Actors from the now-defunct show volunteer their time to attend the festivities, and can be seen hanging out in town with everyone else.

I had arrived a day early in order to get the lay of the land and to do some riding around the area. I got the bike unloaded after checking in and made a phone call to the people that made my LED headlamp that would not stay in place. They told me to send it back, they would send out a new one once they received my old one. Fair enough. Once I had checked my emails, I headed back downtown to the Post Office and mailed off the headlamp. A visit to the local museum, a little sightseeing, some souvenir shopping, a bite to eat at the Busy Bee Café, and some live music at the Occidental Saloon capped off the day…with actor Robert Taylor tending bar!

Me with actor A Martinez

The next morning, I headed out to explore the surrounding countryside, rolling north toward Sheridan, about forty miles away. I started out on I-90, then jumped off onto Highway 14. I wanted to visit the Bighorn Smokehouse and Saloon, which had reportedly been in business since the 1880s. Just my luck, when I rolled up on it, it was closed, and the building was for sale. OK. Off to Plan B. After touring around a bit on some back roads, I headed back to Buffalo, gassed up, and went west on Highway 16 over Powder River Pass toward Ten Sleep. What a great road! Being a state highway, it was very well maintained and featured sweeping turns, grand vistas of the Bighorn Mountains, and a few hairpin switchbacks. Slicing through a section of the Bighorn National Forest, the road climbs over the Powder River Pass at just over 9600 feet, then begins dropping down the shale-crusted mountain and along the Powder River into the Bighorn Basin and the village of Ten Sleep. Although the weather was sunny and mild when I started out, by the time I hit the top of Powder River Pass, the temperature had dropped about 15 degrees and a cold wind was slicing through me. I stopped and put my jacket on, along with some heavier gloves, and motored on. Of course, about fifteen miles down the canyon the temperature began to climb again and was in the mid-eighties by the time I reached Ten Sleep.

Only 250 people or so call Ten Sleep home, but it, like many other towns in this part of Wyoming, is rich in history. One of the main focal points in the small village is the Ten Sleep Mercantile, built in 1907; and is the quintessential general store. I stopped in at the Ten Sleep Saloon for a refreshing beverage and some lunch and learned quite a bit about the town from a couple of locals. The settlement got its name because it was an Indian stopover site on the way from one camp to another, or one destination to another. The tribes in the area measured distances in "sleeps," or the number of times they had to sleep to get to their destination. Ten Sleep was ten sleeps from the Stillwater River in Montana to the northwest; Yellowstone to the west; and Fort Laramie to the southeast. Because of the numerous travelers traipsing through the canyon, the area is rich with archaeological sites filled with artifacts, petroglyphs, and pictographs. Fossils of dinosaurs, plants and sea-life have also been found in the area. More infamously, Ten Sleep was also the location of the Spring Creek Raid in 1909, widely considered the last of the battles in the Sheep and Cattlemen's War. There has always been *(and sometimes still is)* contention between cattle ranchers and sheep ranchers. In March of 1909, cattlemen attacked three sheep herders, killing them and hundreds of their flock. The killers were eventually caught and convicted, but the conflict between sheep and cattle farmers went on for years.

After a great lunch, good conversation, and a personal history lesson, I headed back toward Buffalo and back over the pass. Coming over, I passed a lake just west of the summit that looked pretty inviting, so I made a point to stop on my way back. Meadowlark Lake covers about 200 acres and is clean and clear. It offers fly fishing, hiking, and spectacular wildlife viewing. A lodge sits on one end of the lake featuring cabins and motel rooms. I got a few pictures and headed back to Buffalo. More stargazing *(the TV kind, not the astronomical kind)*, visiting the county museum and talking with other people visiting for the event took up the rest of my day. The next day had an attraction I definitely wanted to take part in: a charity poker run to benefit the Johnson County Animal Shelter in Buffalo, led by one of the actors from the show, Adam Bartley. Bartley, a fellow rider as well as a huge animal lover, decided to raise as much money as he could for the no-kill shelter. In addition to starring in Longmire, Adam is also known for his roles in NCIS: Los Angeles; This Is Us; Vice; and more. Truly a nice guy, very down to earth and personable, he was always willing to talk with people, sign autographs, and just hang out.

The ride started out from downtown Buffalo with Adam riding a new Softail Heritage, leading forty-two bikes. Buy in for the ride was $20. We headed away from town and jumped on to I-25, then I-90 toward Sheridan, hopping off the freeway a mere thirteen miles later to make our way to the Wagon Box Inn in Story. After drawing our cards and spending some time hanging out *(you know how poker runs are)*, we saddled up again and rode to the Lake Stop Resort at Lake Desmet for our second stop. These people pulled out the stops for us: plenty of wait staff, a free do-it-yourself nacho bar, and drink specials for those needing *(or wanting)* a refreshing beverage.

After drawing our cards, we headed back toward Buffalo for our last stop, the Cowboy Saloon where we drew two hands for our cards. The raffle prizes were handed out, and the 50/50 drawing and auction were held. The 50/50 was worth $200, and as luck would have it, I won! I donated my winnings back to the shelter, which everyone thought was so unusual and generous. I don't know about that, where I come from it's something almost automatic to do... in fact, sometimes not doing so can make you feel like a real dick. Auction items were extremely popular with the group, and consisted of artifacts from the show, artwork, and even some personal offerings of Bartley's. Rumor had it that one lady had pledged a $5,000 donation to the shelter, and challenged Adam to raise another $5,000. If he was successful, she would kick in another $5,000. I never could find out if that were true, but when the final tally for the weekend came in, the shelter had indeed raised over $15,000 as a result of Adam's efforts.

It's well known that bikers are generous, especially when it comes to kids and animals. This event was no exception. We always hear about the excesses of actors and stars and their lifestyles, but it's refreshing to meet one who is truly generous with his time and his money. If you follow social media, you will see that Adam is always giving to one charity or another, and the shelter in Buffalo seems to hold a special place in his heart.

Poker run; Buffalo, WY

With the poker run wrapped up, I headed back to Buffalo and grabbed a bite at the Busy Bee Café. That night, Main Street was blocked off and a flatbed trailer was set up in the middle of it as a stage for a street dance, complete with live music. The band was great, a regional band out of South Dakota that played outlaw country, southern rock, and some classic rock. The lead singer is a rider himself, and we had a good time visiting between sets.

CHAPTER TWENTY

After spending five days in and around Buffalo, it was time to move on, and I headed out in the morning over Powder River Pass and into Ten Sleep once again, with my sights set on visiting the Medicine Lodge Archaeological Site on my way to Cody. Rolling out of Ten Sleep on Ten Sleep-Hyattville Road and then on County Road 49, the twenty-five-mile ride was amazing! No traffic, a well-maintained road, and just enough curves to keep it interesting. After a short distance on Highway 52, I came to the Medicine Lodge cutoff and eased my way the next few miles into the site.

There is no "lodge" at Medicine Lodge, but the site is the location of a 750-foot-long sandstone bluff which provided shelter and protection from the elements, with Medicine Creek nearby. Originally homesteaded in 1881 as a working cattle ranch, Wyoming Game and Fish Department purchased the 12,000-acre ranch and created the Medicine Lodge Wildlife Habitat Management Area. Wyoming Parks says that excavations at the site, beginning in 1970, have unearthed petroglyphs, artifacts and signs of human habitation dating back 2,000 years. A portion of the Habitat Management area was turned into the archaeological site in 1973. Petroglyphs, or carvings depicting culture and daily life, are fairly prevalent in the Western United States. They can depict game trails, astronomical events, even territorial boundaries, among other things. Unlike many of the sites, Medicine Lodge is easy to access and even has a campground nearby. Signage depicts when the incisions were made and point out the carvings. Also located at Medicine Lodge is a small visitor center, toilets, and nature trails.

Near Ten Sleep, WY

I headed out of Medicine Lodge westbound on Highway 31, skirted up to Highway 30 near Basin, and joined US-14 for the run into Cody. Since I was into Cody reasonably early in the day, I decided to check out the Buffalo Bill Center of the West. This place is huge! Actually, five museums are located under one roof: The Buffalo Bill Museum, Plains Indian Museum, Cody Firearms Museum, Draper Natural History Museum, and the Whitney Western Art Museum. Founded in 1917 after the death of "Buffalo" Bill Cody, the complex currently covers seven acres and holds more than 5,000 artifacts. The initial log cabin that housed the first museum is now located inside one of the museums in the vast building. Storyboards, exhibits and artifacts from Bill Cody's life are prominently displayed in the Buffalo Bill Museum.

The Plains Indian Museum showcases cultural objects, stories, histories and current lives of the Arapaho, Cheyenne, Blackfeet, Pawnee, Lakota, and Crow tribes, mainly from 1880 to 1930. The

Cody Firearms Museum boasts the most wide-ranging collection of American firearms on the planet, from the sixteenth century to today. The 20,000 square foot Draper Natural History Museum features interactive exhibits, geology, videos and dioramas, and specimens of bighorn sheep, elk, moose, bear, and wolves. Recently updated in 2009, fifty years after its initial opening; the Whitney Western Art Museum features not only works by prominent Western artists, but also replicas of the studios of Frederic Remington and sculptor-painter Alexander Phimister Proctor. There are even interactive exhibits to allow visitors to create their own art.

Hidden from public view is the McCracken Research Library; a collection containing more than 400 manuscripts, over 500,000 photographs, and 30,000 books. In 2008, the Buffalo Bill Center became part of the Smithsonian Affiliates program, which allows them to host artifacts from the Smithsonian Institution, as well as share their exhibits and items with the Smithsonian's museums.

This is not a place to whip in and out quickly. To see everything and experience the complex properly, it would take at least a full day, if not more. I was there for over four hours and still didn't get to see the majority of the exhibits.

I decided I needed to get to my motel and get off my feet for a while, so I made my way down the street to the Western 6 Gun Motel. Yes, that's really the name of it. Nice enough place, but the room was just big enough for a queen bed that I swear was made of concrete and a dresser with a TV on the opposite wall. Even worse, the bathroom was so small that I could hardly fit on the toilet. Okay, I'm not that big of a guy, I stand 5'11" and weigh about 215, but I felt like a damn sardine in this room. Taking a shower with the shower curtain closed was not even an option, so I left it open and used the towels to soak up the spilled water. All this for $105. Welcome to Cody in the summer.

Anyway, after checking into the motel, getting the road grime off my face and the luggage off my scoot, I rode downtown to check out the city and grab some grub. I found this little taqueria along the main drag and decided to check it out. I'm not sure if the young waitress didn't like bikers, or just didn't like her job, but the service sucked… and the food was not much better. Maybe a beer would be good to cap off the day, so I walked down to an open-air bar with some live music. I went up to the bar and stood there, waiting for the bartender to come over. They were pretty busy, but a few of the employees walked past without even acknowledging I was there. Finally, after about four minutes the bartender comes over, looks at me and says, "Do you want something?" The smartass in me really wanted to say, "no, Sparky, I'm just standing here for the hell of it," but I didn't, and I ordered a beer. I handed him a five-dollar bill for my three-dollar beer, he came back with my change and literally threw it at me without so much as a "thank you," "here ya go" or even a "kiss my ass." So much for a tip. I sat outside nursing my beer *(sure wasn't going to try to order another one, ol' Sparky might just shoot me rather than wait on me again)* and decided to head back to my broom closet…I mean, motel room. It just amazed me how terrible the service was and how rude most of the people were, considering Cody is a city that lives off tourism. I'm used to being treated differently or suspiciously as a biker, but it's also not like the good people of Cody don't see many of us. During the summer, this place is loaded with bikes!

No room!

The next morning arrived none too soon and once I was able to get out of bed, I took a long hot shower in the minuscule bathroom. A quick side note: since the crash, I am quite often very sore and my back is very tight in the morning, and it is only made worse by a hard bed…like the one I had in this motel room. A long, hot shower will usually ease the tightness and pain in my back so I can get on with my day. The bed in this room was so hard I could barely get any sleep at all for all the pain, and sadly, there was nowhere else to sit or lie down in that room. I loaded my gear and hit the road, rolling through Yellowstone National Park in the early morning and stopped for a late breakfast at the Grant Village Dining Room. Cowboys and Indians magazine listed the Dining Room as one of the best places to eat in the National Park system. A fifteen-dollar plate of bacon, eggs, hash browns, and toast with a view of Yellowstone Lake helped ease not only my growling stomach, but my attitude as well. The food was mediocre at best, but the view more than made up for any shortcomings on my plate. Coming out of the restaurant, I could feel and smell the rain coming, so I suited up in my rain gear. I made a few more obligatory stops inside the Park, including Old Faithful. The parking lot was jammed, but I tucked my bike in among six or seven other bikes parked near the walkway to the geyser, grabbed my camera and headed in. The rain squall had passed without much fanfare, or me getting drenched, so I shed the rain gear. The famous geyser erupts every forty-five minutes or so and the boardwalk surrounding the site was crowded with other tourists wanting to get a look. Just as I walked up to the railing with my camera in hand, Old Faithful spouted off and spewed a plume about a hundred feet into the air. The eruptions only last about two- to five-minutes, and this was on the shorter end of that range. But I got to see it! I went back to my trusty bike, saddled up, and got out of there before most of the other traffic did. Taking the western road out of Yellowstone is a pain. Arguably the most popular entrance to the recreational area, the last seven miles or so out of the park was a gridlocked traffic jam. Tourists seem to think it is perfectly acceptable to stop in the middle of the lane to look at...whatever. If they do decide to pull onto the shoulder, they still hog half the lane, so passing traffic is reduced to creeping slowly by. And, of course, this goes on in both directions. As a result, the thirty-two-mile ride from Old Faithful to West Yellowstone took me almost an hour and a half.

I rolled out the western end of Yellowstone into the town of West Yellowstone, Montana and into Idaho along Highway 87 past Henrys Lake. The scenic drive along the 6,000-acre lake is stunning as it climbs to 6,800 feet over Raynolds Pass and the Continental Divide back into Montana. US-287 took me north to I-90 and the run into Butte, my stop for the night.

I got checked into my motel, an old motor court style place that looked like it may have been apartments back in the 1930s. Though dated, the room was spotlessly clean and comfortable, a nice change from the nightmare in Cody…and about half the price! I had been having some issues with my laptop the past few days, and while I was downloading pictures from my camera onto the computer, it decided that was a good time to die. Not good. I always carry a laptop with me on my rides, not only to keep up on emails, but mainly to offload the photos from my camera at the end of each day. That way, I can keep track of them as well as delete the ones that didn't turn out, were blurry, or were "what the hell was I trying to take a picture of?" My cross-country trip in 2011 produced over 3,800 photos; there was no way I could ever keep them straight without dumping them into a daily folder. This current death of my laptop was even more troubling: all my photos from the ride so far were on it. Yeah, I know, there are these things called "cloud services" where I can back up my photos and such, but hey, I'm just lucky I know how to use a laptop!

I did some research using my phone and went looking for a computer store in beautiful downtown Butte. The first two on my list were no longer in existence, but a friendly employee at a business where one of the shops used to be told me to go to Staples and told me how to get there. So, off I went. On my way there, I passed a little computer repair place in a converted house, so I pulled in. The guy there took a look at it and confirmed my fears: it was dead. But all was not lost as he said he may be able to resurrect the info from the hard drive. He did say he could likely get the data off the old hard drive and could maybe fix my computer for about $180. The thing was, he couldn't guarantee whether a fix would work or for how long it would last. I figured I should just get a replacement, since that laptop had been bouncing around in my travel bag on the back of my scoot for the last four years or so. He had a few refurbished laptops on hand, so I ended up buying one. Knowing that I was on the road and only in town for the night, he said he would transfer my data from the old drive to the new computer, and I could pick it up first thing in the morning. Excellent customer service…especially since he had told me their current turn-around time on repairs was about three weeks.

After getting back to my motel and having a much-needed adult beverage, I walked up the street a few blocks to an old school burger drive in called Bonanza Freeze. Straight out of the 1950s, Bonanza Freeze was actually founded in 1947. You can't get more American than burgers, fries, shakes and ice cream. Yes, I had one of each: a big sloppy bacon cheeseburger, large onion rings, strawberry shake, and an ice cream cone for dessert. Oh, sure, I could almost hear my arteries slamming shut, but damn that stuff was tasty!

Once back at the motel, I grabbed a chair and was sitting outside my room nursing a cold beer when a guy pulled up in a Ram pickup hauling a trailer. He mentioned something about my bike, and we started talking. The trailer housed an older heavily customized Road King, He was headed from Anacortes, Washington over to Sturgis on a yearly trek. He said he typically goes to Sturgis a week or two before the rally, does all his riding and sightseeing, then beats it out of the area just as the rally starts.

CHAPTER
TWENTY ONE

I gassed up in the morning, stopped by the computer shop, and $400 later I was on the road, my new laptop tucked safely in my T-Bag. I hopped on to I-90 for the 130-mile ride up to Missoula, where I turned onto US-93 and motored up through Western Montana and the Lolo National Forest. About thirty-five miles north of Missoula, US-93 splits with Montana Highway 200 where it joins up with the Clark Fork River and follows the river all the way past Thompson Falls and the Noxon Reservoir into Lake Pend Oreille (*"pond-oray."*) This stretch of road quickly became one of my favorites: solid straightaways, sweeping curves and a few tight corners dominate this well-traveled highway, and the views are often breathtaking and majestic. Other than hitting a five-mile stretch of road construction just east of Thompson Falls, the ride was amazing! I stopped in Thompson Falls for a break and a cold beer, then hit the road again, crossing into Idaho and on to the town of Bonners Ferry, my home for the night. When planning my trip, I had looked at riding up past Flathead Lake, through Kalispell to Libby. I had lived just outside Kalispell for a short time many years ago and have always loved riding along the shores of the massive and gorgeous Flathead Lake. Unfortunately, lodging was unexpectedly expensive even in Libby. My friend Mike and I had stayed at a great little motel in Libby in 2011 on our way home from our cross-country trip for $65. The same motel now wanted $125 for a single room. Way past my budget. So, I started looking in the surrounding area and found that I could get a room at the Dodge Peak Lodge in Bonners Ferry for $67 a night…much more my liking. I'm glad I made the change in my route: Highway 200 was one of the best roads I was on during this entire trip.

Montana Highway 200 near Thompson Falls

After crossing into Idaho and rolling along the northern edge of Lake Pend Oreille, the wind began to pick up, the temperature dropped a bit, and the clouds were looking more and more ominous as I headed toward town. About five miles south of Bonners Ferry I felt the first of large heavy raindrops hitting my exposed arms, but I figured I'd just ride it out since I was so close. It was only five miles, but boy was it a wet ride! The sky opened up with a vengeance about three miles out and I was pretty well drenched by the time I rolled into the motel parking lot. Of course, five minutes after checking in, the sun was back out and burning bright in the late afternoon sky.

Dodge Peak Lodge is a large log-cabin styled lodge with a wing of outdoor access motel rooms attached. It's a very nice place, with super comfortable rooms and a great staff. I checked in, and the clerk gave me a room in the main lodge, upstairs. I went to my room, opened the door, and found a mussed-up bed, towels on the bathroom floor, and full garbage cans. Oops. Back at the front desk, the clerk could not apologize enough and gave me a room in the outside wing of the motel, much more my preference anyway. Dinner that night was at a mediocre sports bar in downtown Bonners Ferry, and I spent the rest of the evening getting the new computer set up and pictures downloaded.

The next morning was sunny as I rolled north out of Bonners Ferry toward Canada. About fifteen miles north Idaho Highway 1 peels off from US-95 and goes to the border crossing at Porthill. Unfortunately, either I was not paying enough attention, or I just plain missed the sign, but I kept going on US-95, which added about thirty miles to my route. The highway took me through an unincorporated community called Good Grief, whose claim to fame is that it was once mentioned on the TV show "Hee Haw" in the early 1970s: "a population of three...two dogs and an old grouch." Don't blink, you'll miss it. I crossed into Canada at Eastport with no trouble, and turned onto BC Highway 3, also known as the Crowsnest Highway. Running a total of about 365 miles along the southern edge of British Columbia, the Crowsnest Highway was an important route during the gold rush in the Similkameen River and the Kootenay Mountains. My plan was to ride the Crowsnest for about 150 miles through the Kootenays and the Selkirk Mountains before dropping south once more into Washington State.

Once over the border, I cruised through the small hamlet of Kitchener and past the Riders Ranch Motorcycle Campground into the town of Creston. I had not had breakfast yet, and I knew that once I was in Canada, a Tim Hortons would appear soon. Sure enough, Creston had a Timmy's along the main drag.

Tim Horton (*1930-1974*) was a professional hockey player for the Toronto Maple Leafs, Buffalo Sabres, New York Rangers, and the Pittsburgh Penguins. In 1964, he opened a small donut shop in Hamilton, Ontario after first trying hamburger and chicken restaurants. An early franchisee, Tim Joyce, partnered with Horton, paying $12,000 to become Tim's partner in what was then called Tim's Donut. Joyce became the majority owner after Horton was killed in a car accident in 1974. Joyce bought out Horton's widow's share of the business in 1975 for one million dollars, becoming the sole owner of the company.

Tim Hortons (*"Timmys"*) is reportedly Canada's largest restaurant chain with over 3,700 stores, and sales totaled 22% of all fast-food revenues in Canada in 2005. Tim Hortons expanded into the US in 1984, and in 1995, fast food chain Wendy's bought Tim Hortons, a partnership that lasted until 2006. In that year, Tim Hortons accounted for 62% of the "coffee market" in Canada and 76% of baked goods sold. Shareholders weren't happy with the merger, as Tim Hortons was outpacing Wendy's, and in 2006 Wendy's began a process to divest itself of the Canadian giant that ultimately would take three years. Tim Hortons was purchased by 3G Capital, also the owner of Burger King, in 2014.

I have long held the belief that it is a crime, not to mention my own personal tradition, to go to Canada and not stop at a Timmy's. When I rolled down that main street in Creston, of course I pulled into the Tim Hortons parking lot. A couple of donuts and a hot chocolate later, I was back on the road, headed west on the Crowsnest Highway once more. The highway climbs, drops, and winds its way through the Selkirk Mountains, and most of the altitudes are fairly low: 5,000 feet or less. That does not mean the views are limited. This road was made for motorcycles; lots of twisties, well-maintained roadway, and spectacular views on almost every turn. I crested Kootenay Pass *(5,800 feet)* and Bombi Summit *(4,000 feet)* before descending into the small city of Castlegar situated at the confluence of the Columbia and Kootenay Rivers, with an altitude of about 1,500 feet. Leaving Castlegar I climbed again into the rugged mountain range, riding effortlessly over Bonanza Pass *(5,000 feet)* before dropping down once more along the shores of Christina Lake. The lake covers approximately ten square miles and is the warmest tree-lined lake in British Columbia.

The early inhabitants of the area, the Arrow Lakes People, also known as Sinixt, valued the lake itself for fishing and left pictographs of their culture in the rocks alongside the lake. Settlers to the region established Fort Colville in 1825, and a Hudson's Bay Company store was established in 1852. Fur trader Angus McDonald, who ran the store, used to travel each year with his daughter and a group of others to Kamloops *(nowadays about a 250-mile journey)*, along the east bank of the Kettle River, crossing the river just below the lake itself. Christina was the bookkeeper for her father, maintaining records and carrying them in a buckskin satchel. They would cross the river on horses pulling a raft loaded with goods. In 1870, the raft on which Christina was riding fell apart mid-crossing, and she was plunged into the fast-moving waters. She was finally rescued and pulled ashore some distance downstream, and still had a grip on that satchel, preserving her father's records. The Council of Chiefs of the Colville Indians later awarded Christina and her heirs the sole right to trap and fish in the area; thereby attaching her name to the lake. She went on to become a successful businesswoman in her own right and is well-known for being the first woman shopkeeper in BC.

The arrival of the railroad in the late 1800s brought more growth to the area surrounding the lake, with numerous towns springing up along the shore. The largest of these was Cascade City with a population of 1,000 people. A dam was built across the Kettle River to provide electricity to the town and surrounding area, but a series of fires in 1899 virtually destroyed the small city.

By the 1920s, Christina Lake had become a popular recreation and fishing area, as well as a popular destination for Americans from northeast Washington who were attracted by the dance halls and saloons along the lake, as Prohibition was in full swing in the United States. A summer resort was built in 1928 and was popular even through the Great Depression in the 1930s. From 1942-49, the hotel was used to house Japanese families as an internment camp of sorts during World War II. The town of Christina Lake continues to be a popular summer resort destination, and is now home to an estimated 1,100 residents. Unfortunately, my fuel level was low, so I begrudgingly pulled into a gas station to top off my tank. Premium fuel was $1.54 per litre (*$5.82 per gallon*), compared to the $3.55 per gallon I was paying in the States. Thankfully, I only had to fuel up once in Canada!

From Christina Lake I climbed once again into the mountains as the road ran alongside the Kettle River. I stopped for an ice cream break at a Dairy Queen in Grand Forks, then followed the highway north around Phoenix Mountain before coming south again through Midway, Kettle Valley, Rock Creek and over the 4,000-foot Anarchist Summit to drop into the township of Osoyoos, 3,000 feet lower. The views from Anarchist Summit of the Okanagan Valley below are stunning: the clear blue lake stretching for miles in either direction, the town spread out along the shoreline, and the rugged mountains off in the distance.

Osoyoos, BC is home to 5,000 people and sits on the shores of the massive Osoyoos Lake. The average daytime temperature in Osoyoos is 62-degrees Fahrenheit, which makes it the warmest town in all of Canada. Summertime temperatures will often reach the upper-80s, with occasional climbs into triple digits. Obviously, the location of the town on the shores of Osoyoos Lake make it a true tourist trap, as well as its proximity to the US-Canada border, a short two and a half miles south.

Anarchist Summit, BC

View of Osoyoos, BC

Osoyoos Lake is huge, eleven miles long with thirty miles of shoreline, and spans the border between the US and Canada. Of its 5,700 acres of surface area, almost 3,700 lies within British Columbia. Water from the lake drains into the Okanogan *(yes, the word is spelled differently in the US)* River in Washington state, then into the Columbia River.

I crossed the border into the United States with some probing questions and long looks from the border patrol officer, wondering why I had only been in Canada for about seven hours. I told him I had entered BC to ride the Crowsnest Highway, and when he asked why, I told him it was because I wanted to, and I never had before. Mr. Border Patrol Agent just didn't seem to understand that. Obviously, he doesn't know a lot of bikers. Once across the border, I found myself in Oroville, a small town just spitting distance from the border, and home to about 1500 people. I spent some time relaxing in the pristine and picturesque city park along the lakeshore before finding a motel for the night. I booked a room at the Camaray Motel, a mom-and-pop run place that by far was the best, cleanest and most comfortable motel I had stayed in on my trip, not to mention the friendliest staff. The Camaray is a motor-court styled motel, with rooms on two floors and a swimming pool. My room was spacious, with a fridge and microwave and even a ceiling fan to keep the air moving. The owner asked if I wanted to wash my bike, as he had a hose-and-bucket set up in the back. Located in the middle of downtown, restaurants and shops were all within walking distance. A number of other bikes from Canada rolled in throughout the later afternoon, and a few of us had some good fellowship sharing our experiences on the road, not to mention a few adult beverages. Having covered a lot of miles the past couple of days, I slept like a log in the comfortable room, and I woke up refreshed and ready to hit the road again. *(Waking up refreshed does not happen often for me, so I am truly thankful when it does.)*

CHAPTER
TWENTY TWO

I hit the road early the next morning...well, early for me anyway. By the time I loaded up my trusty Road King and rolled out of Oroville, it was about 7:30 and I was cruising along under clear blue skies and brilliant sunshine. I was headed south on US-97, a virtual straightaway from Oroville to the town of Omak, about forty miles away. Regardless of the lack of twists and turns, US-97 rolls peacefully through numerous small communities such as Ellisforde, Tonasket, Riverside and more, often running parallel to the Okanogan River, making it a gorgeous ride. I knew I would be getting my fair share of curves and twisties soon, for just south of Okanogan I turned west onto Washington Highway 20 (*SR-20*).

I am not exaggerating when I say every biker in Washington knows about Highway 20; and it's likely that most of them have ridden it at least once. More commonly known as the North Cascades Highway, SR-20 is a designated Washington State Scenic Byway and a National Forest Scenic Byway. The road in its entirety runs from the junction with US-101 on the Olympic Peninsula near the Pacific Ocean and terminates less than a half-mile from the Washington-Idaho border near the town of Newport. What most people know of the North Cascades Highway, however, is the portion that spans roughly 170 miles over the Cascade Mountains from Okanogan to Sedro-Woolley, Washington. It is one of the few state highways that is closed in the winter, due to the fact that the mountain passes can be buried under fifteen feet of snow, and avalanches can be prevalent. The road is typically closed from November to April.

Originally a travel and trade route for the area's Native American tribes, gold miners in the mid-1800s needed a route through the rugged and unforgiving terrain. In 1896, the State Road Commission decided upon what was then known as the Cascade Pass Route, and rough plans began to take shape in 1897. The early roads were continually washed out by flooding from the nearby Cascade River. The Roads Commission then decreed that a stretch of highway was to be built above the Methow (*"met-how"*) Valley, which was completed in 1909. By the late 1930s, two dams had been built along the still-primitive road, and a third, Ross Dam, was being built. Population in the area had continually increased, so a more efficient and modern roadway was needed. The North Cascades Highway Association was formed in 1953, made up of business owners, lobbyists, and politicians; and included plans for old-growth timber harvesting and sales in the dense forest. Five years later, in 1958, the State approved funds to build a six-mile stretch of road from Thunder Arm to the company-owned community of Diablo; as well as improvements to the roads on both sides of the Cascades. Construction was continuous over the next twelve years, and in 1968, President Lyndon Johnson signed the bill creating the North Cascades National Park, which put an end to the use of the highway for timber sales. After more than a century of planning and building, the road connecting the northern parts of Eastern and Western Washington was a reality. The official opening and ribbon-cutting took place on September 2, 1972; with Washington Governor Dan Evans and President Richard Nixon in attendance, taking part in the first official vehicle caravan over the Cascade Mountains.

Climbing out of the Okanogan Valley, the roadway winds its way up into the Cascades to join up with the Methow River near the town of Twisp. From Twisp, it's pretty much a straight shot for about nine miles up to Winthrop. Winthrop is an old west village, complete with wooden sidewalks and false-front buildings. The gold rush of the late 1800s brought the first permanent white settlers, Guy Waring, James Ramsey, and Ben Pearrygin to the area who set up camp at the confluence of the Chewuch (*"chee-wuk"*) and Methow Rivers, creating a small settlement named after Theodore Winthrop, a well-known author and traveler at the time. Waring built a saloon in 1891, but a fire ravaged the town in 1893. Waring's college roommate, Owen

Wister, stayed in Winthrop on his honeymoon and later wrote "The Virginian", known as America's first western novel, after his stay in the town. The novel led to the popular TV series of the same name, which ran from 1962 to 1971. Winthrop was incorporated as a town in 1924.

North Cascades Highway (SR-20), WA

Like many small towns in America, Winthrop was on the decline in the late 1960s and early 70s, but the city saw opportunities for growth when the new highway was completed. Residents Kathryn and Otto Wagner came up with the idea of a Western town restoration, after seeing how the nearby city of Leavenworth had increased their tourism by converting it to a mockup of a Bavarian village. Local businesses and the Wagners themselves paid for the project, which began in 1970. Their desire to design a town as authentic as possible was meant to preserve the "spirit of the valley". The plan worked, as Winthrop is now a popular tourist destination, with cross-country skiing, fishing, hiking, river rafting and other activities offered nearby. It is also home to the oldest legal saloon in the state, Three Fingered Jack's. Reportedly named after a local meat cutter, Jack Lemma, who lost his fingers while working one day, the tavern-restaurant is still in business and thriving. The National Motorists Association dubiously listed Winthrop as number two on its list of "Worst Speed Trap Cities" in 2012. They are right: I saw more cops along SR-20 than I had on my entire journey so far. Part of the reason for the heavy police presence is that the North Cascades Highway, being so popular with riders, has the highest number of motorcycle crashes than any other roadway in the state. According to the Washington Department of Transportation, 20% of all crashes on SR-20 involve motorcycles, with 75% occurring on curves in daylight hours and dry pavement. Inattention and high speeds going into the curves are listed as the primary factors in most crashes. This road does command your attention and focus, but it really is a dream to ride, almost as if it really were created with motorcycles in mind.

As the asphalt cuts through the mountains, it passes several small communities and offers unbelievable glimpses of majestic scenery, crossing the Pacific Crest Trail near the 7,800-foot Whistler Mountain along with views of Diablo Lake and Ross Lake. Clear pristine waters reflecting the lush green landscape surrounding the lakes will take your breath away, and Highway 20 offers many turnouts and scenic viewpoints along the way. Twists and turns abound on the thoroughfare, from moderate sweepers to full-out hairpin sharpies, including a long switchback turn at the south end of the turquoise-colored Diablo Lake. Just past Diablo Canyon, the company-owned town of Newhalem makes for a nice rest stop along the banks of the Skagit River. Owned by the Seattle City Light utility, Newhalem features an information center, general store, hotel, and campgrounds. I took a little break along the river for a soda and a candy bar before continuing west.

Not only was I headed lower in elevation, I was reluctantly headed into civilization as well. Numerous small settlements are located along the western side of the Cascades, including the 12,000 population Sedro-Woolley. Sedro-Woolley is a bedroom community for those working in the larger cities of Mt. Vernon and Burlington along Interstate 5. Not wanting to hit the superslab just yet, I turned north at Sedro-Woolley onto SR-9. While definitely more populated than the areas I had been riding the past few days, it still was much more open than the heavily traveled interstate. My journey for the day was almost finished, as I was in the final forty-five-mile stretch to the city of Ferndale in northern Washington.

When I had initially planned this trip, I was going to ride from Wyoming back home, but then Laura asked if I would meet her in Ferndale for her son's wedding. She rode her bike up from Idaho for the wedding, so I decided to extend my trip to include the festivities, then we could ride back to Idaho together. Once I made it to Ferndale, we met up at one of her friends' house, where we would be staying for a couple of days.

On the way north, she had some issues with her bike blowing fuses and losing her running lights. She made a stop at an independent shop in Tacoma that she had used before, C and A Customs. They looked at her bike and determined what the issue was. The rear tire had rubbed on the wire harness inside the rear fender, so they repaired the problem. They also told her she needed tires, so she authorized them to replace both tires. She hit the road, riding north on I-5. Within fifty miles the problem reappeared. Numerous calls to the bike shop went unanswered, so she asked if I would look at it when I got to her friend's house.

We did the typical rehearsal dinner and family visits that night, and the next morning I pulled her bike into her friend's barn to see if I could figure out what had happened. Initially I thought the brake switch was shorting out, but that proved to be incorrect. Not being able to find the problem, I told her we would load up with fuses, and rather than take our planned leisurely route back over the North Cascades Highway, we would blast down the freeway to Tacoma and get the shop to look at it again.

The rest of the day was spent at the wedding and reception, and by the time we got back to the house, we were beat! The next day was spent just hanging out and relaxing...something I desperately needed. At this point I had been on the road for three weeks and had covered roughly 3,800 miles.

CHAPTER
TWENTY THREE

Monday morning found us loading up the bikes, bidding goodbye to Laura's friends and hitting the road for Tacoma. I had thought about stopping at one of the Harley dealers along the way to see if they could take a peek at her scoot, but being a Monday, they were all closed. We made a few stops along the way to replace fuses and finally got to the bike shop in Tacoma. She went in and told the owner what was going on, he came out, took a quick look at the bike, and said the tire had rubbed through the wiring again. Then he said he didn't have time to fix it.

Wait...what?

He did a repair on the bike that didn't last, and now he won't fix it properly? Laura reiterated that she was traveling, and 500 miles from home, and could not ride it safely. He shrugged his shoulders and said he was too busy, as he was getting ready to leave for Sturgis in a day or so. I was ready to blow my stack, but I made a call to my friends at Dead Center Cycles, and told Jessica what the problem was. She said to bring it down, they would at least take a look and see what was going on. We hit the road for the thirty-mile ride south, pulled into Dead Center Cycles and got the bike unloaded.

Within a few minutes, they had determined that not only had the tire rubbed through the wiring again., but the wiring "repair" done by the other shop consisted of non-weatherproof butt connectors and duct tape. Not only that, but the tire was an oversized tire, taller than the stock application. Laura's bike is a lowered Sportster 1200 Custom, so when she added her luggage to the back of the bike, the taller tire rubbed through the wiring harness. By simply patching the wiring and putting that tire on the bike, it was guaranteed that the same thing would occur. In addition, the taller tire had rubbed on the stud that holds the brake light in place; as a result, there was a groove in the center of the tire.

The guys at Dead Center Cycles repaired the wiring harness *(properly, this time)*, then rerouted it from under the fender to a safer location. The rear tire was replaced with the proper sized tire, and the shocks were adjusted to a stiffer setting.

(Note: Laura sued the first bike shop in Court for the dollar amount of repairs she had paid for and won her case in October of 2020. As of the date of this writing, she has still not received payment from the shop.)

By the time we got done, it was pushing four o'clock in the afternoon, so I asked what she wanted to do: stay overnight and hit the road in the morning, or ride until we didn't want to *(or couldn't any longer)*, then get a place to stay. Great minds think alike, as we both wanted to get away from there as fast as we could. We topped off our fuel and hit I-5 south toward Portland. Fortunately, since it was summer the sun stayed up until almost nine o'clock, so we still had hours of daylight. We hit Portland a few hours later, gassed up again and rolled out on I-84. I was thinking we could call it a day by the time we reached Hood River, about fifty miles east; but we kept going another forty miles to a little place called Biggs Junction. This was one time I was happy to be riding the Interstate, as we both wanted to put as many miles between us and Washington as possible. Not really even a town, Biggs Junction is a census designated place that is home to about 25 full-time residents. Sitting above the Columbia River at the junction of I-84, US-97, and US-30, Biggs is also home to a couple of motels, gas stations/truck stops, a McDonald's, cafes, and convenience stores. We grabbed a bite to eat and got a room in the little motel across the street from the diner, then settled in after what had turned out to be a long, damn day: roughly fourteen hours since leaving Ferndale and 370 miles. That many miles in one day, even though we split it up by spending three hours waiting for Laura's bike to get fixed, absolutely wiped me out. In fact, I was not sure I would be in any shape to ride the next morning. I hit the pillow and was out. Fortunately, the motel was comfy, and I slept like a log *(wait…do logs sleep? If so, do they snore? Oh, never mind…)* and awoke the next morning feeling surprisingly good.

We had a decision to make. Should we ride straight home, 300 miles on the freeway, or take a more scenic route? Since our original plan had been to take three days or so from Ferndale to home, we still had an extra day before Laura had to be back at work. Remember, I really dislike freeways, so anytime I can take a secondary highway or back road, I'm in. Besides, even though I had been away for over three weeks, I was not quite ready to go home yet.

I called my friends Gary and Kelly in Bend and asked them if they were home, and would they be willing to put us up for the night? Gary said that would be great, and we headed south out of Biggs on US-97 for the 120-mile ride. The short day sounded good to me after the long ride the previous day. Climbing out of the Gorge toward Moro was a nice ride, but it was windy as hell once we got onto the plain. We thought we would just take our time and decided to stop for breakfast somewhere along the way. Grass Valley was the first place we came to with a café…but it was closed. Next came the small ghost town of Shaniko. From previous trips though that part of Oregon, I knew they had an old hotel and café there. Yep, it was closed too. We finally stopped in Madras and grabbed a late breakfast at the Black Bear Diner.

Shaniko, OR

We reached Gary and Kelly's house just about noon, and since Gary wasn't going to be home from work until about three o'clock, we took off again and rode down to Todd Lake and Lava Lake near Mt. Bachelor. One of my favorite rides in Central Oregon, Laura had never ridden it. Part of the sixty-six-mile-long Cascade Lakes Scenic Byway, the two lakes are only a couple of dozens of such lakes nestled in this part of the Cascade Mountains. Coming west out of Bend, the first thing we saw was the majestic Mt. Bachelor, standing 9,000 feet above the landscape. Even though it was late July, the ancient volcano still had some snow on its flanks. A couple of miles past the ski area, we pulled onto a short dirt road that took us to Todd Lake.

The lake was calm, clean, clear, and stunning in its beauty. It sits at an elevation of 6,100 feet, and the still waters of the lake reflect the dense, lush forest surrounding it. From the parking lot to the lake itself is a small hike, but very easily traversed, even for me. We hung out at the water's edge for a little bit, then saddled back up and headed for another stop, Lava Lake.

Lava Lake is actually two lakes; Little Lava Lake and Big Lava Lake *(very clever, these names)*. A private campground with a small general store and docks with boat rentals sit on the shore of the almost 400-acre lake. We grabbed a drink at the store, walked onto the dock and I sat with my feet in the water enjoying the peace and quiet of the water...especially after the hectic activities of the day before.

We made it back to Bend just as Gary got home, and we spent the evening visiting, laughing, eating, and drinking.

There was nothing special about the next day on the road: 325 miles of straight out riding across the desert of Eastern Oregon. Well, riding is always special to me, but there were no exquisite scenic overlooks, no interesting monuments...just riding. We stopped at a little café for a bite and continued on into the town of Hines for gas. The temperature was climbing from the chilly temperatures of the morning and was now in the high eighties. From Hines, we cruised through part of the Blue Mountains and into Vale, Oregon, where we decided to top off the tanks once more *(Laura's bike needs gas about every 150 miles)*, and since it was mid-afternoon, we thought we should just grab a late lunch/early dinner and take a break. The diner we chose was a great place to eat: good food, super friendly wait staff, and reasonable prices. It had been a great day on the road, nice and easy riding with no problems.

Until we went to pay. Laura couldn't find her wallet, so I went out to see if it was on her bike or in the saddlebag somewhere. No luck.

She looked through all her gear and pockets for it too. No luck. She called the gas station in Hines to see if she had left it there when we gassed up, but nobody had seen it. We had also stopped in Juntura, to shed some more of our gear in the climbing temperature and hydrate with some water, so she thought she may have dropped it there.

So…off we went, blasting across the fifty-five-mile ride back to Juntura to look for her wallet. No luck there, either. That sucker had seemingly disappeared from the face of the Earth.

We got back to Vale, topped off our fuel again since we had racked up 110 miles or so since we were in Vale a couple of hours ago, and headed home. *(Side note: she got a call a couple of weeks later from someone who said they found her wallet and was going to mail it to her. They never did.)* The rest of the sixty-mile trip home was uneventful, but with the extra side trip to look for her wallet, it made for a day well over 400 miles, and I was in pain!

I parked in the garage, walked in the house, grabbed a beer, and stripped and went out to the hot tub. Yes, it was 100 + degrees out, but damn that spa felt good! Unpacking the bike could wait for a while. In all, I had racked up over 5,300 miles since leaving home twenty-three days earlier.

CHAPTER TWENTY FOUR

As you can easily tell, for me it's all about riding. Since the crash, my PTSD shows itself as anxiety, fatigue, and outright depression at times. My constant chronic pain adds to that depression. Those who live with chronic pain will tell you that not only is it depressing, it is exhausting. There are still days when I don't open the curtains, don't go outside, don't talk to anyone, because it simply takes too much effort to do it. The mind-numbing pain coupled with those days of sheer exhaustion are hard to describe, but I remember a line from Shakespeare's "The Tempest": "Hell is empty and all the devils are here." OK, that might be a little over-dramatic, but it gets my point across.

The effects of the brain injury are occasionally even worse. Three things I have always been good at are reading, writing, and riding *(not necessarily in that order)*. The brain injury robbed me of my ability to concentrate and a lot of my memory, even to this day. My struggles with reading and writing are getting better, but it has taken years to regain only a part of what I could once do. There are still times that I cannot recall the word I want to use, or I lose my train of thought in mid-sentence. To say the least, it is frustrating. Prior to my injuries, I loved to do crossword puzzles. Even now, I still cannot do even the simplest of them.

The other thing I was good at, was riding motorcycles. Thank God I still am. But riding motorcycles requires a lot of concentration and focus. Of all the exercises, games, and tricks I have used to try to "rebuild" my brain, riding has proved to be the most beneficial. Riding is therapy, it is freedom, it is release from anxiety and worry, it is relaxation. When I am in the saddle, I am in control and can let the worries, fears, and anxieties melt away. I honestly believe that if I could not ride, I would have ended up in a rubber room at the giggling academy long ago. And since the ride is everything, planning rides has been a challenge as well. Long gone are the days when I could just ride until I wanted to quit. Long gone are the days when I could rack up 500 or more miles tooling down solitary country roads. Before the crash, my friend Lori and I rode from Reno to Tacoma in one day, 720 miles or so, and never gave it a second thought. My trip planning now averages about 250 to 300 miles per day. There are times, such as Laura's and my trip from Ferndale to Biggs Junction, or Bend to home; that blow that out of the water, but I do my damnedest to keep those to a minimum. For example, the ride home from Bend. Due to unforeseen circumstances, that day ended up clocking in at 422 miles. The good thing was, I had nowhere to go and nothing to do the next day, so I had my recovery time…and it did take me two days to recuperate from it. Rolling a 350-mile day can be done, but I may not be in any condition to do it again the next day.

I've typically been a person who can find or see the good even in bad situations. Let's face it, most of life's challenges are temporary. No, I'm not some Little Johnny Sunshine, more like a grumpy old fart, but good things can come from bad circumstances. The crash in 2016 changed my life in ways I could never have imagined. But it was also a blessing in many ways.

I also believe that everything happens for a reason, even if we never know what that reason is. My Dad was diagnosed with prostate cancer in 1982. Fortunately, the doctors discovered it early, he had surgery and treatment to rid himself of the disease and was cancer-free until his death in Decmeber 2021. In 2012, my older brother had an aortic aneurysm that burst. He should have been dead before he hit the floor, but for some inexplicable reason, he made it to the hospital, underwent surgery to repair the damage with a Kevlar aorta and new heart valve, and is once again one of the healthiest people I know. My crash in 2016 was, obviously, almost fatal. I have no reason for living through it other than by God's grace. The only thing that ties all these incidents together? At the time that we each suffered our challenges; we were all 58 years old. I most likely will never know the "why," but I am eternally grateful that we each survived.

The fact that I am still alive and reasonably healthy is a blessing, and I believe due to the grace of God. I am able to live alone, be self-sufficient, and while I am not rich by any means, I have *(usually)* enough money to do the things I want…like travel. Since I can no longer work, I can go whenever I want…at least, when my body and brain allow it. There are people who have asked me, "if you can ride, why can't you work?" It's a valid question, but the answer is not so simple. In bare terms, I cannot work because of my pain. My jobs prior to the crash were physical, demanding positions. I can no longer drive professionally, as drug tests are required, and I will fail every test I take. Most other employers will require drug tests, so that takes me out of the market. In addition, my bad days can often show up without warning. Those days render me virtually unable to get off the couch, as the pain level is so intense that just moving can bring me to tears. Thank God, those days are getting fewer, and are less than when I lived in Washington *(I now live in a drier climate),* but they still happen as many as four or five days a month. The pain is only part of the picture: all-out fatigue will hit without warning as well, and I end up sleeping most of the day away. No employer is going to give me that much sick time. My focus and concentration still suck, and almost every job I have ever had has required me to be able to lift fifty pounds. Yeah, that's not gonna happen.

But I live for the ride.

I can do, and have done, rides without any planning at all. Just pick a direction or flip a coin, and I would be gone! Those excursions turned out to be some of the most fun, most exciting, and most memorable. But deep down, I am a planner. Especially now, with my limited range, I plan trips out to compensate for my weaknesses. Planning also helps with my mental processes: I make myself pay attention to the little details and thereby improve my cognition, memory, and attention span.

I now especially prefer small towns over large cities, back roads over freeways, and solitude over crowds. That's not to say these plans are carved in stone, because anyone who has done any bike trips will tell you, plans can change, and often will. There's an old saying, "Want to make God laugh? Tell him your plans." It's true. A broken throttle cable in Kansas, an electrical breakdown in Washington, a lost wallet in Oregon, a road block in the middle of Nowhere, Colorado…these can all throw you off your game plan. The trick is, just roll with it. Hope for the best, plan for the worst.

CHAPTER
TWENTY FIVE

Meanwhile, the legal wrangling from the crash continued. Remember, as part of Mr. Applonie's *(shithead's)* "sentence," he was required to pay restitution to Laura and me. His meager payment of a combined $25 per month was ludicrous. Every month, I got a check from the Court for $14.93, Laura got the other $10.07. As the total amount of restitution ordered is not being paid in full, the Court charges 1% interest on the unpaid balance, which means that the amount he actually owes goes up every month. We saw this as his way of saying "fuck you" to us and the Court and decided to do something about it. At that point, he owed us about $70,000.

I contacted an attorney that specializes in collections and garnishments and began to investigate the process of garnisheeing his wages. Normally, it's not a big deal: in simple terms, the attorney takes the judgment to the court clerk, gets the information on where the debtor works, and serves notice of garnishment. The employer then deducts whatever is allowed by law from the debtor's paycheck before he receives it and sends the money to the Court for disbursement. The attorney obviously gets a fee for his participation, but Laura and I figured that was okay, since we would at least get something more than $25 each month.

As usual, there was nothing normal about this process, either. Since the Court Judgment for restitution was attached to a criminal case, everything had to go through the Court itself, with hearings and appearances before the Judge., Of course, shithead tried to fight it, to no avail.

Over the next few months, our attorney tried to get court dates, hearings, paperwork, and all the other necessities done to get our money. Then Covid hit. Court was cancelled, non-essential motions were put on the back burner, and everything came to a halt. When things finally did open back up, the Court was in no hurry to do anything...it took another four months to even get the authorization from the Court to find out where shithead worked.

All this wrangling was essentially an exercise in futility: garnishments are only good for a short period of time, so the attorney has to keep going back to the Court for authorization to file a new round of garnishment. We each did finally get a couple of checks in late 2020 for small chunks of what was owed to us, but the battle continues. And his balance keeps rising. That $70,000 owed to us is now over $88,000 and counting. I do know we will likely never see it, unless he sells his house, in which case the Court will collect due to the lien on his property. But I'm also not one who gives up. To add insult to injury, Court-ordered restitution is only good for ten years, so in 2027 we will have to go back to Court to renew it.

CHAPTER TWENTY SIX

It wasn't long after getting back from my three-week long trip that I was itching to hit the road, and especially after dealing with all the legal bullshit. I wanted at least one more trip before summer was over. I started looking at my maps and thinking of places I hadn't been yet, and a new ride began to take shape.

Near the city of Twin Falls, in south central Idaho, are numerous waterfalls and natural attractions. I put together a plan to ride mostly back roads over to Twin Falls, then spend a day chasing waterfalls. I decided I would take three days or so to go play, and on a Sunday toward the end of September, I loaded up the bike and headed out. I should have recognized the obvious omen: the day before I left, it was 90 degrees, the next day the mercury struggled to reach 65 under cloudy skies.

I wanted to avoid the boredom of the superslab as much as possible, so I headed out Highway 78 through the high desert terrain, with scrub and sagebrush as my view. I passed through a couple of the small towns that inhabit this stretch of Idaho highway, and eventually joined up with I-84 near Hammett. Almost as soon as I hit the freeway, the skies opened up and the rain came down with all the force it could muster. Thankfully, I had stopped and put my raingear on before getting on the freeway, but that didn't make the ride much better. Not only was the rain relentless, but the spray from other cars and semis was blinding. I only needed to run the freeway for about thirty miles, but it was a long, torturous, and dangerous ride.

My first scheduled stop was Malad Gorge State Park, and by the time I reached the exit, the rain had slowed to an annoying drizzle. Entering the park, the Ranger looked at me like I was crazy for riding in this kind of weather...not the first time I've encountered that! The 250-foot-deep canyon was carved by the Malad River, which flows through the 450-acre park and tumbles down a sixty-foot waterfall into the Devils Washbowl before emptying into the Snake River.

Malad Gorge, ID

The sun was finally making an attempt to break through the heavy cloud cover, and since the rain had stopped, I was able to shed my rain gear. My next stop was Miracle Hot Springs, and I thought a nice hot soak in the mineral springs would do my body some good.

Miracle Hot Springs was founded in 1960 and contains fifteen individual baths, six VIP baths, and two outdoor pools with waters reaching 103 degrees. Floods in 1984 almost wiped out the resort, but the family rebuilt the pipeline and well feeding the pools. Surprisingly, the water has none of the typical sulphur smell that is so common with hot springs. When I reached the site, however, I discovered they were closed on Sundays. Figures.

With tears in my eyes and a heavy heart *(OK, not really, but it sounds good in the story)* I headed for my third and final stop of the day: Niagara Springs State Park. The road to the park cuts through rich verdant farmland, with a mile and a half stretch leading to the park entrance itself, known as Niagara Springs Grade. The steep twisting Grade wound down into the Snake River Canyon and was announced by a sign at the beginning of the descent: "Pavement Ends."

Damn.

Sure enough, the road turned to gravel and dirt, which of course was muddy from the recent rainstorm. As if that weren't enough, the road was steep, narrow, and without guardrails. I contemplated my situation for a moment, but since there seemed to be no other vehicles going down or coming up, I kicked my scoot into gear and headed down. A half-mile later, the road turned to pavement again as I approached the Niagara Springs Fish Hatchery. Yay!! Oh, but then it turned back to dirt once more a few yards later. Damn. I was committed by now, and wanted to see the springs, which actually presents as a waterfall cascading out of a rock wall at the base of 350-foot cliffs. The water charges out of the wall at about 250 cubic feet per second, coming from the snow melts of the Big and Little Lost Rivers, located near the Craters of the Moon National Monument. From the park, the waters empty into the Snake River close by. Park Rangers will say that the water can take up to 200 years to reach the springs. A little further exploration into the park led me to Crystal Lake, a gorgeous alpine lake covering about fifteen acres, extremely popular with fishermen and hikers.

By now the sun had made an appearance and it was a respectable 72 degrees out, and I headed into the community of Buhl for the night. I stopped at a nice-looking place called the Oregon Trail Inn, a clean and inviting motor court motel. My room was really comfortable and spacious, with free wi-fi and even a free breakfast the next morning. The owners of the motel, Sidney Howard and her husband Todd Fahner, are locals who had lived in Portland for many years before buying the motel. They are super friendly and welcoming, in addition to being riders, and we had a great visit talking about our adventures.

Cloudy skies and cooler temperatures greeted me the next morning, and after a free breakfast of biscuits and gravy *(Food of the Gods, you know)*, I headed out to explore the countryside. The evening before, when I was looking for a place to have dinner, I saw a small sign that said, "Balanced Rock, 17 miles." I found the sign and headed through the farmland and into a box canyon along Salmon

Falls Creek. In typical Idaho fashion, the landmark was not indicated by any signs or markers, and while I was cutting through the twisties in the canyon, I almost blew right past the parking area. Yep, they were right, it's a balanced rock. But impressive, nonetheless, as it is a forty-eight-foot-high, forty-foot-wide boulder weighing an estimated forty tons, sitting atop a perch thirty-six inches by seventeen inches. Pathways lead up to the base of the structure about 200 yards off the road. It's amazing what the wind ripping through the canyon can create.

Balanced Rock; near Buhl, ID

Two more waterfalls were on my radar that day, Perrine-Coulee Falls and Shoshone Falls. According to my maps, Perrine-Coulee Falls was inside the city limits along the Snake River Gorge, which slices through Twin Falls. Again, no markers, signs, or indicators as to exactly where the Falls were made it a challenge to find. I even resorted to using my phone's GPS *(have I mentioned I hate GPS? OK, just checking...)* which gave me an idea of where to go, but still not an exact location. I finally was able to locate an overlook with a view of the Falls by walking a short way down a paved pathway on the edge of the Gorge. Waterfalls are really neat, and some are even impressive, this one was just kinda cool. *(I later found, on a subsequent trip to Twin Falls, that there is another access offering a better view)*

Shoshone Falls was next. At least this one had signs pointing the way, and it took no time at all to get there. Known as the Niagara of the West, Shoshone Falls is 500 feet wide and over 200 feet tall... taller than Niagara Falls; and one of the tallest waterfalls in the United States. I paid my five-dollar entry fee, rode the short road down the hill into the parking area, and grabbed my camera. Even though I was there in late September, the flow of water cascading over the ledge was impressive. One of the park employees told me the estimated flow was about 400 cubic feet per second. Spring is the best time to view the Falls, with snowmelt from the mountains creating a volume as high as 12,000 cubic feet per second roaring down the rocks into the canyon.

Not far from Shoshone Falls, and accessible by a one mile walk on a pathway that is not well-marked *(big surprise there)*, is the site where motorcycle daredevil Evel Knievel made his famous attempt to jump the Snake River Canyon in 1974. Only the mound of earth that the launch ramp was built on remains, so I headed to the Visitor's Center along US-93, where there was allegedly an Evel Knievel Monument commemorating the event.

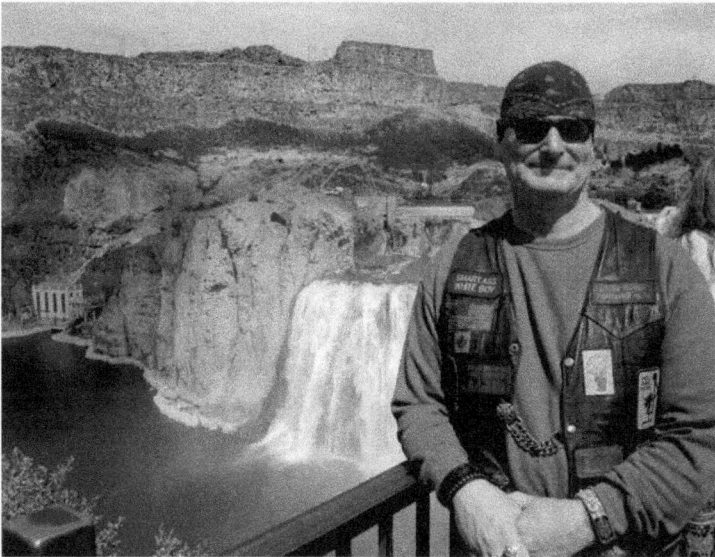

At Shoshone Falls, ID

Nothing was there. I went into the Visitor's Center to ask about it, and the volunteer on duty said the monument used to be in the parking lot, but vandals destroyed it years ago and it was finally removed. He did spend a few minutes recalling the infamous attempt and showed photos of the ill-fated jump. Using a custom-built rocket-powered "motorcycle," Knievel wanted to jump the one-mile width of the canyon. Unfortunately, his jump failed when his parachute allegedly malfunctioned, opening just at the point of takeoff. Rumors persist that Knievel pulled the 'chute manually, but no one knows for sure. The vehicle landed on the bank of the Snake River directly below the takeoff point. Another stuntman, Eddie Braun, successfully jumped the Canyon in 2016. The dirt ramp is still visible from the Visitor's Center, and while still accessible, recent reports say the mound is used as a backstop for the Twin Falls Police Department's shooting range.

Most of the clouds had dissipated and the temperature had climbed to a comfortable 75 degrees by the time I rolled north out of Twin Falls on US-93. A short distance later, at the town of Shoshone, the road became Idaho Highway 75 and started its ascent into the Sawtooth Mountains. As I headed further north, I was also heading up, climbing from about 3700 feet to Sun Valley at 5800 feet. This was an impressive and relaxing road to scoot merrily along, with no real major challenges but plenty of panoramic scenery and lush forest. Once I passed through Ketchum *(Sun Valley)*, I continued my ascent and finally pulled over at the 8700-foot Galena Pass to put some more clothes on...I was freezing! I donned my chaps, heavy coat and heavy gloves and headed the remaining thirty miles into the town of Stanley.

Stanley is truly a resort town, with a full-time population of less than 100 and smack in the middle of the Sawtooth Mountains. I got a room in the Mountain Village Resort *(it's called a "resort" so they can charge more than if it was just called a "motel")* and was given a small wooden chit good for a free drink in the bar. What a coincidence! I was ready for a refreshing adult beverage...or five...after my ride. I unpacked the bike, cleaned the road grime off my face and headed over to the bar. The place was not terribly busy: three of the tables filled with various customers, a couple of guys at one end of the bar watching a baseball game, and another couple toward the other end of the bar. I went in, sat at the bar, and for the next five minutes watched the bartender/server walk back and forth, refill the guys' drinks at the end of the bar, walk past me again to take someone's order, grumbling about something on his way back to the kitchen.

After another couple of minutes, I got up and walked out. Never did get a "hi, be right with ya," "sorry for the wait," or even a "bite me." Hell, he wasn't even that busy!

Instead, I got on my bike and decided to explore the tiny village. The main drag through Stanley is paved, but that's about it...most every side road is still dirt and/or gravel. I found a small bar-restaurant called the Kasino Club and went in to get a beer. I mentioned to the bartender that it looked like the town was starting to close up for the winter, and he told me the population drops to about twenty people. "It's like 'The Shining' up here in winter," he told me. As luck would have it, they had a dinner special that night: an eight-ounce pork chop with a bourbon/brown sugar glaze, baked potato, salad bar and veggies...all for less than $20. The service and the food were fantastic! I stopped at the little market across from my motel and grabbed a beer, then went back to my room to finish off the day.

Despite the bad service and overpriced room, the motel was actually comfortable, and I woke up the next morning looking forward to the ride home, 160 miles of mountain roads and incredible scenery. When I went out to unlock the bike and get my stuff loaded, I got a surprise: thick fog encased the town, and a rime of frost covered everything! Granted, Stanley sits at 6,200 feet, but I was not expecting ice. I went back into my room and pulled up the weather forecast on my computer: 30 degrees. My route home was going to take me even higher into the mountains over the 7,000-foot Banner Summit before dropping into Garden Valley, so I figured I had better hang out for a bit before heading out. I rode across the highway to the local gas station, not only to fill up the tank, but to see how slick the roadway was. A truck full of construction workers said the road between Stanley and Lowman was not bad, "a few" icy spots but easily passable.

I went back to the motel to grab a quick breakfast and hung out in my room for about an hour and a half before deciding to brave the elements and get my ass home. I suited up in my heated gear and rolled out of Stanley, and in a few miles had climbed above the clouds to be greeted by a gorgeous bright blue sky and brilliant sunshine. By the time I had crossed over the pass and headed into Lowman, the temperature had warmed to the point where I could shut off my heat. I made the turn onto Highway 17 and began my descent along the Payette River and into Garden Valley. The meandering nature of the river dictates the course of the road, with sweeping curves and a few tighter turns for the first twelve miles or so. I crossed Grimes Pass *(4,800 feet)* and dropped into Garden Valley for the run out to Highway 55. Once again, the road follows the river into the town of Horseshoe Bend, where I was able to shed some of the heavier gear as the temperature was now in the mid-sixties. A turn onto Highway 52 took me along the river once more as I rolled into and through Emmett for the final stretch home.

CHAPTER TWENTY SEVEN

As I began writing for the various magazines I occasionally sent stories to, as well as my own website *(Hiwayflyer.com)*, I reflected on my trips over the past two summers. As I mentioned earlier, my days of racking up mega-miles on the road are over, and multi-day trips are done with the understanding that I may have to stick around an extra day if my back decides to ramp up the pain level to eleven.

But the other thing that came as a pleasant surprise…or rather, realization…was that I am no longer in any type of a hurry. It's no longer a priority to get from Point A to Point B as soon as possible. If I don't get on the road at the crack of dawn, oh well. If I don't get off the road by two or three in the afternoon, oh well. I will get "there" when I get there. With that realization, I also noticed another level of freedom. Like I said before, I can usually see the better side of things, and the results of the crash have not been all bad. Not having to work leaves me open to planning trips when I want, without necessarily having to be back in two days, or even two weeks. A day trip prior to the crash, that encompassed 350 miles, I will now plan for two days or more if there is something or somewhere worthwhile to explore.

As a society, we have been trained to be in a hurry. Everything must be done with an urgency, from rushing to get to work in the morning, to buying that particular item on sale *(today only!)* or to binge watch the latest "it" series on TV. Our attention spans have gotten shorter…why do you think TV commercials are mostly thirty seconds or less? Even television news stories are fed to us in ten-or fifteen-second clips. We are an instant gratification society, and not only do we want it all, we want it NOW.

My shift in attitude took me some time to get comfortable with, because I was that guy who had to do everything right now (*in the interest of full disclosure, I still am in many ways*). But being on the road, being in no hurry, and slowing down enough to see things I normally would have missed is a true blessing. Yes, I will throw in the trite saying that life is precious.

We often give little or no thought to our own mortality, that is, unless or until we are faced with it. I thank God for every day that I have on this planet, even though some days are dark, depressing, and excruciatingly painful. But even those are tolerable because tomorrow will be better.

My winter was spent adding improvements and personal touches to my bike, planning rides, and working on various small projects. The area in which I live is subject to snow and bitter cold in the winter months, so riding is not always a possibility. Cold weather itself doesn't keep me out of the saddle, but if there is snow or ice on the roads, my trusty Road King is resting in the garage. Rain is another thing: as I have gotten older, and with my injuries more affected by damp or wet weather; I can and sometimes will ride in the rain, I just don't want to. Getting caught in a rainstorm while riding is one thing, heading out for a day ride in a downpour is quite another.

One of the trips I had planned for the following summer was a jaunt into Canada, then down to Sturgis. A friend of mine had moved to the infamous city and offered a free place to stay during the rally. I had been to Sturgis once in 2006, and really didn't care if I went again (*you know: been there, done that, got the t-shirt*), but I decided a free place to stay and a chance to visit an old friend were too good to pass up. I wanted to go to Canada, specifically Saskatchewan, to go to the city of Saskatoon. My Mother was born there, and her family were early settlers there…in fact, her family was among the first white settlers in the province. I had been to my Dad's birthplace of Calgary, Alberta years before, but never had been to my Mom's hometown. There are numerous places in Saskatoon that are rich with our family history, and I planned to ride up there, take a few days to explore, then head down to Sturgis just in time for the rally.

I prearranged my route, made a couple of reservations for lodging, and did my research. The dates were set, my friend in South Dakota was notified, and I was ready to roll.

And then it happened. The now-infamous Covid-19 pandemic hit, the country shut down, and life came to a grinding halt. The border between the United States and Canada was closed, with no timeline to reopen. As the months wore on, it began to look like my trip was not going to happen.

I try to not let certain things bother me, I'll just roll with it and move on. Unless you start messing with my rides…then I get pissed!

The trip was planned for early August, and by late May I decided to scrap the idea of going across the border and started working on Plan B. The city of Sturgis had decided to go ahead with the rally, rather than shut it down. A smart move, as cancelling the rally would have decimated that community's economy. Instead of going north into Canada, I decided to head east into Grand Teton and Yellowstone National Parks, spend a couple of days fooling around in the park, then rolling into Sturgis…avoiding freeways as much as possible. The government had reopened the parks, but many of the services and tourist attractions were still closed or limited.

The other trip I had planned was kind of an extension of my Grand Canyon trip the year before. After leaving the Grand Canyon area, I had thought about riding down to Winslow, Arizona but scrapped the idea at the time, because it would have made for a 450-mile day, and as you know by now, I cannot do those. I devised a route to take me to Winslow, but then where should I go? The state of Colorado was beckoning once more, and I opted to go ride Pikes Peak. By the time I had finished the ride plan, I would spend about two weeks rolling through the Western United States.

CHAPTER
TWENTY EIGHT

Winslow, Arizona is a typical, dying American small town. In its heyday, Winslow was the largest community in northern Arizona, due to its proximity to the railroad lines, the famous Route 66, and the Navajo and Hopi Reservations. Rumor has it that Jackson Browne travelled through Winslow and found himself standing on a corner in downtown Winslow. He later wrote the song, "Take It Easy," with Eagles singer Glenn Frey, which featured the line "I'm standin' on a corner in Winslow Arizona, it's such a fine sight to see. It's a girl, my Lord, in a flatbed Ford slowin' down to take a look at me." The song would become, in 1972, the first of the Eagles' many number one singles. In the late 70s, the construction and expansion of Interstate 40 bypassed many of the old portions of Route 66, Winslow included. With no traffic passing through, the town withered and began to die. Shops and businesses closed and sat empty. The municipality seemed to be stuck with a dwindling population.

In 1997, the Standin' on The Corner Foundation was formed to create a memorial to the song that had mentioned the now dying town. Dedicated in 1999, the park consists of a bronze statue depicting a musician with his guitar *(modeled after the sculptor's son)*, a two-story mural on a false storefront wall, and a statue of the late Glenn Frey erected in 2016 as a memorial. More often than not, there is a 1950s era Ford truck parked at the curb as well. The shoulders of the statues are polished bright by the people who have stood with their arm around the musician for photo ops. I would have loved to have seen Winslow in its prime, as there are just enough remnants and reminders of the businesses from the "glory days" of the early 1960s. Now home to about 9,000 people, Winslow depends on the tourism of the small park, which draws over 100,000 people each year. Most of the downtown businesses are abandoned or boarded up, the streets are empty, and only a couple of restaurants have survived.

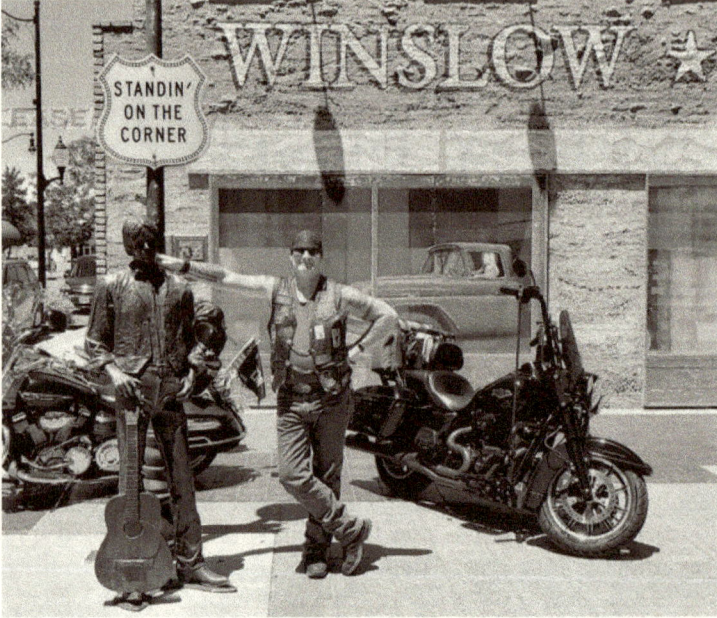

Standin' on the corner...

Across the street from the Park, and kiddy corner to it, are a couple of stores selling everything a tourist could want: trinkets, Route 66 merchandise, Eagles CDs and posters, snacks, drinks, and so on. One store plays an endless loop of Eagles tunes through its outside speakers. A giant replica of a US Route 66 highway sign is painted in the middle of the intersection. Sadly, if not for the memorial, I think Winslow would simply disappear into the surrounding desert as a victim of our hurried lives.

After spending the night at a time-worn but cozy motel in Winslow, I wound my way north into Colorado, eventually making it to Cañon City. I had been riding in and skirting rain for most of the day, and about fifty miles west of the city, near Salida, the rain intensified. Torrents of water were drenching the road, which made it exceedingly difficult to see. Since I only had a short way to go, I figured I would just tough it out, so I kept pushing on...until the hail started. Pea-sized hail was bouncing off everything in sight, including my bike and my helmet. So much for toughing it out. Even the cars and trucks on the road were pulling off. The problem was, there was no place to hide. I finally came across an abandoned café and pulled off the road. The only shelter I found was a grizzled old tree that did almost nothing to protect me, but I hunkered down and laid across my fuel tank. After a few minutes, the hail began to let up and cars were getting back on the road. I cautiously started my scoot and headed east toward town in the driving rain, which dried up completely just before I hit Cañon City. Of course, the sun was out and the temperature had climbed into the high-70s by the time I got to town, and I got some very strange looks as I rode through the city toward my hotel, fully ensconced in my rain gear. My plan was to stay for a few days while I explored the area, which included a ride up toward Colorado Springs and Pikes Peak.

I had heard about a scenic road near Cañon City called Skyline Drive, and set out the next morning to find it. Located on the edge of town, Skyline Drive was conceived in the early 1900s as a plan to build a road along the hogback ridge overlooking the area. Sixty inmates from the nearby Colorado State Penitentiary *(the Cañon City area is home to seven prisons, as well as a decommissioned Women's Prison)* began work on the road in 1905. The narrow two-and-a-half- mile road was completed in 1906, and the city council designated certain days for vehicle traffic and others for horse-drawn traffic. A stone archway at the beginning of the route was built in 1932, again by inmates, using stone quarried from forty-five states in the US. Because of its narrow width, only about fifteen feet at one point, the road is a one-way thoroughfare which rises 800 feet to a scenic overlook offering a panoramic view of the landscape below. There are a few places where the roadway drops off steeply on both sides...and there are no guardrails. Fortunately, I was there fairly early in the day and there was no other traffic to contend with, other than joggers and walkers attempting to tackle the hill. It was a hair-raising start to the day, but spectacular.

From there I rode up to an old mining town called Cripple Creek, which sits at about 9,500 feet elevation and is now home to 1,100 people. The once-bustling town was founded during the gold rush days of the 1890s. In 1896, a fire ravaged the small city, burning half the downtown to the ground. Another fire erupted four days later, destroying what was left of the charred business district. The resolute townspeople rebuilt the town within a few months, and many of those 1896 buildings are still in use today. Mining is still a big business around Cripple Creek, with small claims actively operating. As of 2005, more than 23 million troy ounces *(roughly 68,600 pounds)* of gold had been pulled from the hills surrounding the town. Visible on the hills is the huge complex owned by Newmont Mining. Operating 24 hours a day all year long, it is the second largest producer of gold in the world, after South Africa.

Skyline Drive: near Cañon City, CO

On my way back to Cañon City, I made a stop at the Royal Gorge Bridge not far from town. A 360-acre Park was built around the Royal Gorge Suspension Bridge, which spans 1,260 feet across the Arkansas River, more than 1,000 feet below. Admission to the park is not cheap: $27 per person. Built in 1929 and costing $350,000 *(the equivalent of over $5.5 million today)*, it was the highest bridge in the world until 2001. It remains the highest bridge in the United States, and one of the ten highest in the world. Two 150-foot towers anchor the suspension cables that support a steel substructure, covered by 1,300 wooden planks. Many of the attractions in the park are on the far side of the Gorge, accessed by an aerial tramway. Among the attractions are a zipline, snack bars, concession stands, a small Amphitheatre; and the "Skycoaster": a simulated free-fall ride that takes riders 1,200 feet over the edge of the chasm. The walkways throughout the park are paved, so it is fully accessible.

In 2013 a wildfire erupted on the western side of the Gorge, and managed to jump the massive crevasse, damaging or destroying 90% of the park attractions and buildings. Surprisingly, the bridge itself suffered the least amount of damage, with about 100 boards scorched by the fire. The admission fee was well worth paying, as the views from the park and the bridge are breathtaking, not to mention dizzying!

I spent the rest of the day exploring and riding many of the backroads and small towns before cruising back to my motel and planning my next day's ride: Pikes Peak.

Originally named "Highest Peak" in 1806 by famed explorer Zebulon Pike, it later became known as "Pike's Highest Peak." The United States Board of Geographic Names *(yep, it's a real government agency)* officially renamed it "Pikes Peak" *(without the apostrophe)* in 1980. The mountain is situated in the Front Range of the Colorado Rockies, rising 14,115 feet above sea level, and is the highest point in the contiguous United States east of its location. It often can be seen from 100 miles to the east. Edwin James was the first American to climb the mountain in 1820. Katherine Lee, a writer and professor, took a trip to the summit in July of 1893. The stunning views from the top led her to write the song, "America the Beautiful." In 1913, a race car driver named William Brown decided to drive his car up Pikes Peak, a trip that took him five and a half hours to traverse the nineteen-mile route. It wasn't until the 1950s that the first stretch of road up the mountain was paved, and then only six miles of it was completed. It remained that way until 1998, when the Sierra Club filed a lawsuit on the grounds that continuous efforts to keep the gravel and dirt road to the summit functioning was irreparably damaging the surrounding environment. Years of legal wrangling ensued before a settlement was reached and paving the remainder of the road was finally completed in 2012.

While it didn't take five and a half hours to ride to the top, it did take a while, partially due to other traffic, but also due to the terrain and layout of the road itself. This road is a challenge, a thrill ride, and an experience like no other. I paid my entrance fee and headed out from the kiosk behind a couple of other bikes. The road was pretty tame: nice sweeping curves, a few sharper corners, and the occasional short straightaway, all on well-maintained and smooth pavement. I could feel the temperature drop from the comfortable 75 degrees at the base as I climbed in elevation. Along with the increase in elevation came the change of terrain. Thick lush forest and verdant meadows became thinner and sparser, and about nine miles up the nineteen-mile journey, it became evident that things were about to get interesting. The roadway narrowed, the turns became sharper and came more often.

Pikes Peak Road

Sheer drop-offs with no guardrails were on my right, hairpin turns and switchbacks were constant, and at the 12,000-foot timberline the trees disappeared, the temperature dropped, and the incline increased drastically. Coming into some of the sharper corners, all I could see was sky as the road bent out of my field of vision. Vertigo-inducing drops plunged a thousand feet down in many places. The last stretch of the climb is known as the Manitou Incline, a 4,000-foot length of road, dominated by sharp turns and hairpins, that climbs 2,000 feet in elevation before reaching the parking lot at the sixteen-mile mark. On the day I was there, that was as far as we could go, as construction at the summit was limiting traffic. Fortunately, there were shuttles running to take people to the summit and the Visitor's Center. The good news was, the shuttles were running every five minutes; the bad news was, there was a little over an hour wait for each shuttle. Once I was on a shuttle, the three-mile trip to the summit took another twenty minutes. The temperature at the summit was drastically different than down below, a cold wind was slicing through everything and my phone showed it was 48 degrees. Some clouds were moving across the sky, which limited the view a bit, but the sights from the top are breathtaking! Even with all the construction equipment and projects blocking some of the viewpoints, to stand on that mountain and look out is unbelievably awe-inspiring. No wonder Katherine Lee was inspired to write a song. I could see for miles in every direction; and on clear days it is said that a person can see not only parts of Colorado, but New Mexico, Utah, Kansas, and Arizona, as well as the curvature of the Earth! *(Take that, flat-earthers!)*

I could see thunderstorms off in the distance heading our way, and as I climbed aboard a shuttle for the ride back, a few fat raindrops dotted the windshield as we made the white-knuckle ride back to the parking lot. Oh, don't get me wrong: the driver was extremely cautious, the ride was slow, and he was very attentive to the narrow, serpentine roadway leading back to the parking lot. But, sitting in the seat closest to the sliding door, with someone else driving, on a narrow road...my anxiety was ramping up despite knowing I was safe, so let's just say I was glad to get back to the parking lot!

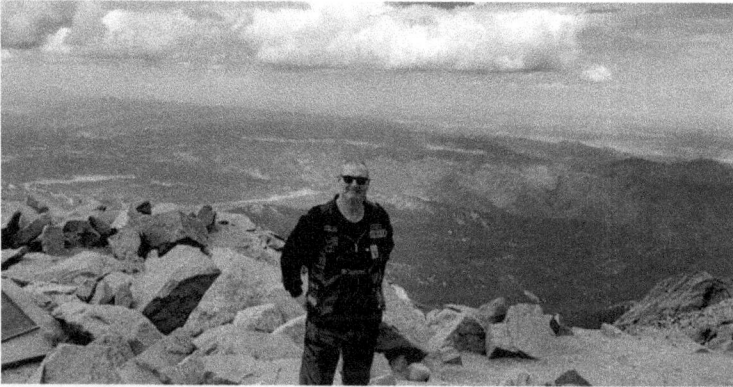

Pikes Peak summit

Somehow, I had managed to stay with the bikers I had ridden up the hill with, and we all proceeded to head back down, before the late afternoon thunderstorm rolled in. It's not unusual on the mountain to have storms suddenly show up, seemingly out of nowhere and without warning, so when we saw the clouds coming toward us, we wanted to beat it out of there. Well, "beat it" is an exaggeration, as our trip down the mountain was as dizzying as the ride up. We all saddled up and began our descent. In some ways the ride down was more harrowing than the ride up, as the drop-offs that had been behind us coming up were now directly in front of us as we negotiated the sharp turns on the snakelike road...and remember, no guardrails or barriers. For the first ten miles or so of the drop, I never got out of second gear as the combination of traffic and topography prevented anything remotely resembling speed. In addition, I didn't want to use my brakes any more than necessary, as it is not hard to burn out or overheat your brakes on a road like this. Once I got below the timberline and closer to the entrance, I was able to increase my speed a bit, but since the area is rife with wildlife, the speed was still slow. I believe I never got above 35 miles per hour on the entire jaunt down to the Ranger's kiosk.

Back at the entrance *(exit?)* to the park, I shed my helmet, coat and heavy gloves since the temperature had climbed to a comfortable 75 degrees as I came down the mountain. After a quick bathroom break and goodbyes to my recent traveling companions, I was on my way back to Cañon City for the night.

CHAPTER
TWENTY NINE

I got home from my Winslow-Pikes Peak trip without incident, twelve days and roughly 3,300 miles after leaving home. I cleaned and serviced the bike, got caught up on my laundry and other household chores then loaded up the bike eight days later for the next adventure: Grand Teton Park, Yellowstone Park, and Sturgis.

Laura was going along on this ride, and we headed east on a bright, clear, and warm summer day. Our destination was Idaho Falls, across the state from my house, and we made a stop at Craters of the Moon National Monument along the way.

Heading out of Idaho Falls the next morning, we got about five miles out of town and Laura said a couple of warning lights had come on. We pulled over and I noticed it was the check engine light and battery/charging system light. I made a few quick checks to the battery cables and the connection at the voltage regulator, pulled the trouble codes, and found a charging system fault. I thought maybe one of the connections may have been loose, so I checked a few of the external connectors. I didn't find any that were obviously loose, so I cleared the codes. I fired up the bike and noticed the charging system light was off. We rode back into Idaho Falls and Grand Teton Harley-Davidson to see if they could at least check it out. Thankfully, the lights did not come back on as we made it to the dealership. Of course, being the week of Sturgis, the store was packed with bikers coming and going, and the service department was slammed with travelers. I explained to the advisor what had happened, he said they would get to it as soon as possible.

This is one great thing about traveling: if you have an issue, the dealer will *(most of the time)* go above and beyond to get a look at the bike. I've only had one really bad experience with a dealer while traveling, in Duluth, Minnesota. I had a charging system failure coming through Wisconsin, and we headed for the nearest dealer, which happened to be in Duluth. We got there on a Saturday just as they opened, and I told the service advisor what had happened. All I asked him to do was diagnose it, so I could call it in to the extended warranty company and get a motel. He wouldn't even look at it. I explained that we were traveling, roughly 1,700 miles from home, and all I needed was a diagnosis…a job that normally takes about a half-hour. He was adamant that they "would not even look at it until Tuesday, and we probably don't have a stator in stock anyway."

A little explanation: The problem I was having with that Road King was a very common issue for that era of Harleys. The stator would short out and usually cause the voltage regulator to fail as well. It's similar to the alternator going bad in a car. Every dealer I know of carries these parts in stock as they replace a lot of them. The other thing to know is, when I worked at a Harley dealership, we always did our best to at least look at and diagnose a traveler's bike, no matter how busy we were. The times I had to call a regular or local customer and let them know their bike was not going to be done because we had to repair a traveler's bike, I was never met with any opposition.

When he said they wouldn't even look at it, and gave me the bullshit line about the parts, I was livid. I went up front to look for my buddy, and of course a salesman attacked…. I mean, greeted us. Nice guy, actually, and upon hearing of my predicament, he directed us back across the river into Wisconsin to a small independent shop called Color and Chrome. We headed off, found the shop, and told the owner my predicament. Not only did he get my bike in, he called in a tech on his day off, had his wife run and get the parts *(from the aforementioned Harley store … who woulda guessed?)* and got my bike back on the road by mid-afternoon.

Anyway, back in Idaho Falls, it took a couple of hours, but they gave Laura's bike a good looking over, and decided there was nothing wrong, the charging system checked out. The tech said I may have inadvertently fixed it when I checked the connections. Both our bikes performed beautifully the next couple of days on the way to Sturgis.

Of course, we did the normal tourist activities in the Black Hills: Crazy Horse, Needles Highway, Devil's Tower, Vanocker Canyon, and downtown Sturgis. We did have one day of just lying about and relaxing, as my back was barking at me pretty good from all the riding and activity. My buddy, Michael, took us up into the Black Hills on his side-by-side and showed us views and parts of the area most people never get to see…it was awesome!

Sunrise at Devil's Tower, WY

People who know me, know I hate freeways. Okay, maybe "hate" is a little over the top, so let's call it an intense dislike. It's not because my crash technically happened on a freeway, it's because freeways have no soul *(when I use the term "freeway," I'm typically referring to Interstates).* They were designed to streamline traffic and make travel more efficient, but they characteristically slice through the countryside like a scalpel through skin. Boring, tedious, and mind-numbing, I will do my damnedest to avoid freeways when I am on my scoot, unless I have no other choice, or I am in a time crunch to get from Point A to Point B. I had been poring over maps and playing with Google maps, and decided we were going to ride the 1047 miles home without touching a freeway. Yes, I have been accused of being obsessed with staying off the superslabs when I am on my bike, and that's okay. To each his own, right?

We rolled out of Sturgis on a beautiful sunny morning, rolled up to Deadwood and stopped to fill up our fuel tanks. Laura mentioned her bike was making a ticking noise, so I took a look. The oil was full, but when she started it up, I heard it…tick tick tick. Further inspection found one of the exhaust flange nuts on the back cylinder was missing. I called my buddy, and we shot back down to his house… it was easier to go the fifteen miles back to his house than try to do a repair in the gas station parking lot. I got out my tools and dug through my buddy's junk drawers *(all of us old guys have cans or boxes of miscellaneous screws, nuts, bolts and whatever),* trying to find the right sized nut, to no avail. We made a quick run to the local True Value hardware store, bought a couple of the nuts I needed, and went back to the house to make the repair. Half an hour later, we were once again on our way.

We sailed easily back up through Deadwood and Lead, merging onto US-85 at Cheyenne Crossing and riding into Wyoming. Wyoming's name came from an Eastern Algonquin language, and was originally used in the Wyoming Valley of Pennsylvania. It is reported to mean "big river flat." Maybe it should have meant "wind never stops." Don't get me wrong, I love Wyoming! It is a gorgeous state, with everything from desert landscape to towering mountains. But I have never ridden through Wyoming without getting clobbered by the wind. There is even a mountain range in western Wyoming called the Wind River Range. This day was no exception. Our ride between Newcastle and Casper on Highway 450 and 387 was brutal. Not only did we fight a hard-hitting headwind all the way, but we hit the grasshoppers…or should I say, they hit us. These nasty little kamikazes were hitting us, our bikes and anything else they could think of. By the time we made it to Casper, we were tired, sore, and covered in grasshopper guts.

The next day took us west past the 16,000-acre Pathfinder Wildlife Refuge on Highway 220. We then jumped onto Highway 287, Highway 28, and finally US-191 for our run into Rock Springs. *(Future ride idea: US-191 runs from Douglas, Arizona near the Mexican border all the way north to the Canadian border north of Malta, Montana.)*

The wind had finally settled down to a light breeze and we back-tracked up US-191 the next morning through an inviting little Mayberry-looking town called Pinedale, where we stopped for a quick snack and for Laura to top off her gas tank. Just north of Pinedale, we met up with the Snake River just south of Grand Teton National Park. We turned onto US-89/US-26 and rode into Idaho along one of the most beautiful roads I have ever been on. The asphalt ribbon twisted and curved through the Caribou-Targee National Forest with amazing views of the river and the Palisade Reservoir. The eighteen-mile-long reservoir was created by the construction of the Palisades Dam in 1957 and now covers over 16,000 acres when full. It seemed to go on forever, as the road followed the contour of the shoreline. Past the reservoir, the landscape was dominated by lush farmland and pastures. We made our way to Rigby, a small city of 4,200 people just north of Idaho Falls. There were limited options for lodging, but we found a Motel 6 that is truly one of the nicest ones I have stayed in. Unfortunately, the only food options in the town were fast food joints, but the desk clerk told us they did have a Domino's Pizza, so we ordered dinner from there, and went next door to the convenience store for beverages and snacks while waiting for our delivery.

The next morning was bright and mostly clear, with only a few fluffy clouds dotting the sky...but damn, it was cold! With the temperature barely reaching 40 degrees, we left Rigby in our rear-view mirrors and began our journey home. We bypassed Idaho Falls and headed west on US-20. This is a pretty desolate stretch of highway across the Idaho desert, and while the mercury had climbed a bit, it was still pretty chilly. As we passed the Idaho National Laboratory, it weirdly seemed to warm up considerably. Once past the complex, it cooled down again. Why is that weird? Well...

The Idaho National Laboratory *(INL)* started out as an artillery range in 1941, just after the attack on Pearl Harbor. After World War II, the facility began to grow and change, and is now perhaps best known for building the prototype reactor for the world's first nuclear powered submarine, the USS Nautilus. Now covering over 900 square miles, many organizations have built more than fifty nuclear reactors on the site, and it now contains the largest concentration of nuclear reactors in the world, employing over 4,000 people.

Just past the vast INL site, we motored into the town of Arco, and decided to stop for breakfast. In 1955, Arco became the first city in the world to be powered completely by nuclear power. A little roadside café called Pickle's Place provided us with a great breakfast and a relaxing rest before rolling past the Craters of the Moon National Monument and into the city of Mountain Home, along I-84.

In keeping with my idea of not riding any freeways, we crept through town, turned onto Idaho Highway 67, and rolled past Mountain Home Air Force Base before joining Idaho Highway 167 into Grand View. Idaho Highway 78 took us the remaining miles toward home.

Looking back over the trip, our journey would have only been seventy-seven miles less had we taken the freeways…and a lot less fun!

CHAPTER THIRTY

As I write this, it has been just over five years since that crash. Everything has changed since that day, but not necessarily for the worse. I still struggle daily with the effects of my injuries, the constant pain, the ongoing issues from the brain injury, and the anxiety caused by the resultant PTSD.

Laura also deals with chronic pain daily, as well as the residual effects of her injuries. More surgeries may be in her future, she is taking a "wait-and-see" attitude about that. She is back at work, but her job as a Surgical Technician is much harder to do as she is unable to stand for hours on end during the procedures, and her ten- to twelve-hour days just wipe her out.

But I am able to ride. My riding is much different than it used to be, but I still ride. I will ride until I am no longer able to, or until I am dead. Like a patch on my cut says, "ride til you rot." I no longer ride 400 or 500 miles in a day, but I still ride thousands of miles every year…it just takes more of an effort and takes me longer. Every ride I take, I give thanks to God that I am able to still get my knees in the breeze.

I'm alive, I'm riding, I'm back on the road. In other words: I am home.

On the road again

THANKS TO:

- Lori Chapin & Tammie Nelson (my "angels")
- Elaine Smith
- Dwight Mikkelsen
- Jeremy & Jessica Ruse and the crew at Dead Center Cycles, Lacey WA
- Laura Hartsock
- The Nurses and aides at Tacoma General Hospital
- The Staff at Orchard Park Health and Rehabilitation Center

ABOUT THE AUTHOR

Bryan Hall was born and raised near Portland, Oregon; and has lived in Oregon, Montana, Washington and Idaho. Born with a terminal case of wanderlust, he has ridden his motorcycle all over the United States, Alaska and parts of Canada; and has traveled to Mexico and the Caribbean. He currently rides a 2018 Harley-Davidson Road King and is on the road every chance he gets. His book, Life Behind Bars, was published in 2013. He has written for numerous motorcycle magazines, as well as his own website, hiwayflyer.com. In 2020 he launched his own You Tube channel, hiwayflyer. He is the proud father of two grown daughters, one granddaughter, and four grand-dogs.

You can contact Bryan by writing to him at hiway@hiwayflyer.com